Project Management
in Construction

Project Management in Construction

ANTHONY WALKER MSc, PhD, FRICS

Professor of Building,
The University of Hong Kong

COLLINS
8 Grafton Street, London W1

Collins Professional and Technical Books
William Collins Sons & Co. Ltd
8 Grafton Street, London W1X 3LA

First published in Great Britain by
Granada Publishing 1984 (ISBN 0-246-12199-8)
Reprinted by Collins Professional and Technical Books 1985

British Library Cataloguing in Publication Data
Walker, Anthony
Project, management in construction.
1. Construction industry – Management
2. Industrial project management
I. Title
624′.068′4   TH438

ISBN 0-00-383161-2

Typeset by David John Services Ltd, Maidenhead, Berks., U.K.
Printed and bound in Great Britain by
Mackays of Chatham, Kent

Contents

Preface

My interest in how the construction industry manages projects on behalf of clients was aroused many years ago when I was engaged in practice. It seemed to me that we adopted a standard approach irrespective of the great differences between projects and clients, often with predictably poor results. Subsequently, the management of projects received more attention from clients, the professions and industry but this tended to concentrate upon developing procedures, techniques and technology. What did not receive sufficient attention was how we might best organise and manage projects to take full advantage of the skills available for the benefit of our clients.

I was able to undertake research in this area and consequently felt that there was a need for a book that examined the nature of the project management process in construction. The book therefore focusses upon the way in which the people involved in projects are organised. Construction projects nowadays can involve a host of different professionals and specialists: the architect, engineer, quantity surveyor, estates surveyor and specialist subcontractors, as well as the general contractor and client. Their integration and co-ordination and the resulting decision-making process are fundamental to effective project management.

This book is designed to provoke those involved in the process to reconsider, analyse and improve the effectiveness of the organisation structures used in the management of construction projects. Its basis lies in the systems approach to management and it distils the ideas central to such thinking and applies them to construction. The book is concerned particularly with the integration of the contributors to the process and the way in which decisions are made. The client's role in this process is distinguished and examined. A model of the construction process is developed, as is a method of analysing and designing project organisation structures. Against this backcloth a variety of organisational forms available for the implementation and management of construction projects are considered in terms of their contribution to the fulfilment of the client's objectives.

This book does not pretend to cover the whole field of construction project management. Techniques, procedures, etc. are well covered elsewhere and behavioural aspects need a separate treatment. However, in developing a systems view of organisation, the interface of these and other aspects cannot be ignored and is referred to in relation to the analysis and design of organisation structures.

All authors need stimulus and assistance and I suspect that I needed more than most. I am therefore extremely grateful to colleagues and friends for their help and guidance: in particular to Alan Wilson and Arthur Britch, who helped me to develop my initial ideas; to both staff and students in the Department of Surveying, Liverpool Polytechnic, for their observations; to the Science and Engineering Research Council, for their recognition of the need for research in this area and for providing funds for mine to continue; to Paul Hodgkinson, who transformed my rough sketches into elegant drawings and corrected them on the way; to Pat Johnson, who typed what many would describe as an unreadable draft, and to Paul Johnson who worked hard correcting my wayward grammar; and especially to my wife, for her forbearance and encouragement, particularly when things were going badly. Nevertheless, the responsibility for any faults that remain is solely mine; there would simply have been many more without the assistance of those whose help I gratefully acknowledge.

Anthony Walker

1 Relevance of Organisation Structure

INTRODUCTION

The management of construction projects has been carried out since man first co-operated to erect buildings yet there is little documented knowledge of how people interact in this process. It is revealing that historical and contemporary accounts of construction work pay little attention to how people worked together and managed their activities.

Writers over the ages have concentrated upon the buildings themselves, particularly on aesthetics, the use of new materials, technological developments and the impact of buildings on their environment. How people were organised and managed has received scant attention. What has been written has tended to be about such charismatic characters of enormous ability as Brunel and Wren, and not about how they structured their organisations. Refreshing in this respect is Alan Wilson's contemporary account[1] of how the construction of Rhuddlan Castle was managed by Master James of St. George. He completed the works using 3000 men in less than three years, and that was over 700 years ago. Perhaps we would see a significant improvement in performance if the managers of the construction process today were given titles like 'Master James'!

The way in which the available skills are used is of paramount importance in providing what clients expect from their buildings. There is little point in the construction industry developing the special skills of its members if no one is going to amalgamate them in the best manner to meet a particular client's objective.

The conventional method of organisation for construction projects, by which is meant one in which the architect or engineer is designer and manager of the process, using specialist consultants with the construction contract awarded by competitive tender after the design is substantially complete, evolved in response to pressures other than solely the needs of clients. It developed in conditions that were considerably more stable than those faced today by both the construction industry and its clients.

The complexity of the conditions within which the construction industry's clients exist makes them place increasing demands upon the industry in terms of the performance of projects (both functionally and aesthetically), the capital and running costs and the time required from conception of the project to occupation. This has come about as a result of technological developments, uncertain economic conditions, social pressures, political instability, etc. Within such conditions, clients have to increase their effectiveness to remain competitive and to satisfy their own clients who transmit the demands of a complex world to them. (Competitiveness can be seen to apply to public as well as private clients − see chapter 4.) The construction industry has in turn to respond to demands from clients that arise from such conditions and is itself also subject to external pressures in a manner similar to that of its clients. It therefore needs to respond by mobilising the talents it possesses in a way which recognises the particular needs of individual clients. It is unreasonable to suppose that the conventional way of organising construction projects is likely to be a universal solution to producing a project in today's conditions.

The complexity of clients' demands, together with the increasing complexity of building, civil and industrial engineering, and other constructional work, particularly as a result of technological developments, has over the years resulted in specialisation within the construction industry. The professions associated with construction have emerged as separate skills (e.g. architecture, quantity surveying, structural, mechanical and electrical engineering, acoustics, hygiene), as have the many specialist subcontractors working with the general contractor. On any project, even a small one, a large number of contributors and skills are involved. On the largest there is a vast range of skills and materials required and an enormous variety of people and equipment to mobilise. Where these projects are carried out overseas, there are many additional problems of logistics and language.

The key to the management of construction projects is therefore the way in which the contributors are organised so that their skills are used in the right manner and at the right time for the maximum benefit to the client. There is little point in the construction industry developing its skills if they are not then implemented effectively.

The way in which the industry and its skills and professions have evolved has compounded the problem of organising effectively.

Specialisation has been accompanied by the creation of independent companies offering the specialisations, and the complexity of construction has led to greater interdependency between the specialisations and hence between companies. This produces a high level of differentiation within the construction process and a consequent need for strong integration of the independent companies and skills. This situation has been reinforced by professional allegiances which, in the U.K. and elsewhere, have been compounded by the establishment of professional institutions, which in turn have contributed to the division of the design professions among themselves and their separation from construction firms.

It is against this background that the conventional solution to project organisation has attempted to cope with increasing complexity and uncertainty. The strain has shown in recent years through the increasing use and development of alternative approaches such as design-and-build, management contracting, construction management and 'alternative methods of management'. What these approaches have not provided, however, is a framework for designing organisations to suit the particular project and the conditions in which it has to be executed. The pressure from client bodies is now making the professions and industry take more seriously the need for organisation design, which is fundamental to the improvement of the project management process.

MANAGEMENT AND ORGANISATION

Before discussing project management and particularly organisation structure, it is necessary to have a clear idea of what is meant by management and by organisation. It is hardly surprising that definitions of management have occupied authors of management literature at length when the *Shorter Oxford English Dictionary* lists ten meanings of 'to manage', ranging from 'training a horse', and 'wielding a weapon' to 'controlling the course of affairs by one's own action'. The minds of many are also conditioned by its ironical use, which the dictionary quotes as 'to be so unskilful or unlucky as to do something'. Much of the literature presupposes that the reader has a clear idea of the concepts of management and organisation. Some writers offer a dictionary-style definition, but the operational definitions offered by Cleland and King[2] are perhaps the most useful.

An operational definition is one that identifies a number of observable criteria, which, if satisfied, indicate that what is being defined exists. Cleland and King's operational definition of *management* identifies the criteria of 'organised activity, objectives, relationships among resources, working through others and decisions'. In providing an operational definition of *organisation*, Cleland and King had to employ many of the elements used in their management definition. Organisation and management are intrinsically interlinked concepts. The former is concerned with the 'organised activity' part of their definition of management, and their observable criteria are 'objectives, some pattern of authority and responsibility between the participants with some non-human elements involved'. Decisions, both routine and strategic, are required from management to make the organisation operate.

Although management and organisation are closely interlinked concepts, it is interesting to note that management is more frequently defined in the literature than is organisation. Yet it has been said[3] that 'how best to organise the efforts of individuals to achieve desired objectives has been one of the world's most important, difficult and controversial problems'. It may be that, in industries more homogeneous than the construction industry, the distinction between management and organisation is sufficient, but an especially sharp focus on the organisation of the many diverse contributors to construction projects is necessary if the successful management of projects is to be achieved.

For the purpose of accomplishing a construction project, an organisation can be said to be the pattern of interrelationships, authority and responsibility that is established between the contributors to achieve the construction client's objective. Management is the dynamic input that makes the organisation work. When this takes place, the organisation ceases to be static and works and adapts to meet the objectives laid down for it. Management is therefore concerned with setting, monitoring and adapting as necessary the objectives of the project organisation as transmitted by the client, and with making or advising on the decisions to be made in order to reach the client's objectives. This is achieved by working through the organisation set up for this purpose, which is particularly difficult for construction projects owing to the temporary nature of organisations. In many cases, members of the organisation are part-time, as they are also involved in other projects and are normally seconded from their parent company.

The contributors to the project act through the organisation that has been established to carry out their work, and they produce information that allows the managers of the project to make the decisions that will keep the process going. The effectiveness of the organisation structure is therefore fundamental to the quality both of the information on which decisions will be taken and of the decision-making process itself.

DEFINITION OF CONSTRUCTION PROJECT MANAGEMENT

General management definitions require amplifying before they can be used for defining construction project management, which can be said to be:

> The planning, control and co-ordination of a project from conception to completion (including commissioning) on behalf of a client. It is concerned with the identification of the client's objectives in terms of utility, function, quality, time and cost, and the establishment of relationships between resources. The integration, monitoring and control of the contributors to the project and their output, and the evaluation and selection of alternatives in pursuit of the client's satisfaction with the project outcome are fundamental aspects of construction project management.

In this context, resources is a general term, which includes materials, equipment, funds and, in particularly, people. A fault with many current definitions of project management is that they focus on 'managing a project' and do not make specific reference to managing people to achieve a project. Although it can be implied that projects can only be achieved by working through others, nevertheless it is important that definitions make explicit reference to this fundamental aspect of project management.

The implementation of this definition could take many forms in practice, depending on the nature of the project and the circumstances in which it is carried out. However, as referred to earlier, the professions tend to seek to achieve it through a conventional organisation structure. Nevertheless, no matter what organisation structure is adopted, if project management is taking place, the activities identified within the definition should be observable.

OBJECTIVES AND DECISIONS

Reference to objectives and decisions has been predominant so far and they have particular significance for construction project management. The objectives of the project management process are those of the client, and a role of project management is to ensure that the project organisation works to achieve the client's objectives.

Similarly, decisions taken during the process should be taken with the sole purpose of achieving the client's objectives.

Because a large number of organisationally independent firms are usually involved in construction projects and second their staff on a part-time basis, their integration and orientation to the client's objectives are major functions of project management. Thus, objectives need to be clearly stated and the head of the project management team will have to extract them from the client, state them clearly and transmit them equally clearly to the contributors to the project.

It is important that any adaptation of the objectives that may subsequently occur is treated similarly. It is natural to be greatly concerned with the original objectives, but adaptations are not always given the same attention, leading to dissatisfaction with the completed project on the part of the client.

As contributors will normally be involved in a number of projects at the same time, conflicting demands upon their time and attention are always likely to occur within contributors' firms. The project organisation must be designed and managed to resolve such conflict in the interest of its client so that it does not detract from the achievement of the client's objectives.

THE PROJECT MANAGEMENT PROCESS AND THE PROJECT MANAGER

The use of the title 'project manager' in the construction industry has deflected attention away from consideration of the process of project management. It is necessary at this point to distinguish between the titles and the process. A common reaction seems to be that if there is someone called a project manager, then all project management problems will instantly be solved. But the project management process will take place irrespective of the titles of the people in the process. The industry needs to be concerned with identifying and studying the process of managing construction projects and with structuring its organisations and implementing techniques and procedures that make the process more effective. It may well be that the designation of a suitable individual with the title of project manager will assist in this, but it is not likely to be an instant and universal solution.

The approach should be to identify the process to be undertaken for the achievement of the specific objectives of the client, the conditions in which it is to be carried out and the people available for the project. As a result of this analysis, the organisation structure should be designed to suit the particular project. The nature of the project should establish the roles of the contributors and ascertain whether or not a role emerges that requires the title of 'project manager' is a reflection of the project's needs. Such an approach would focus attention upon the process of project management with the result that effort should be put into making it more effective rather than into a preoccupation with titles.

The title 'project manager' should have a reserved meaning in the construction industry. Projects are executed for clients and as the title means managing the project as a whole, then it should refer to managing the project for the client: that is, the specific and unwavering objective of the project manager must be achievement of the client's objectives. The project manager will therefore seek to resolve conflict in the process in the interests of the client. This implies that the project manager should be a member of the client's organisation.

One step removed from this, and more practically, the project manager could be acting as a professional consultant without an entrepreneurial interest in the project. Even in this latter case it is possible to conceive of a situation in which the project manager might have difficulty in resolving conflict solely for the benefit of the client if, for instance, he is handling a number of projects that generate conflicting demands on his time and attention. Any further removal of the project manager from direct responsibility to the client makes the title difficult if not impossible to justify.

The title does not always have this reserved meaning in practice and this leads to confusion. Other titles are available which can be used to imply the orientation of the particular management activities undertaken. For instance, construction manager, contract manager, design manager are roles that are often designated project manager. The activities implied by such titles do not necessarily have the client's interest as their main concern. It must be added that they do not, of course, deny satisfying client objectives as being one of their objectives.

To complete the array of management activities in the construction industry, it should be recognised that general management of the contributing firms will also be taking place, the objective of such activities being the effectiveness of the firm.

PROJECTS, FIRMS AND CLIENTS

CONFLICTING OBJECTIVES

The work of firms in the construction industry and its professions presents two types of management issue: the problem of managing firms and that of managing projects. This leads to a rather complex kind of matrix management structure, shown in a much simplified form for a conventional arrangement of contributors in fig. 1.1.

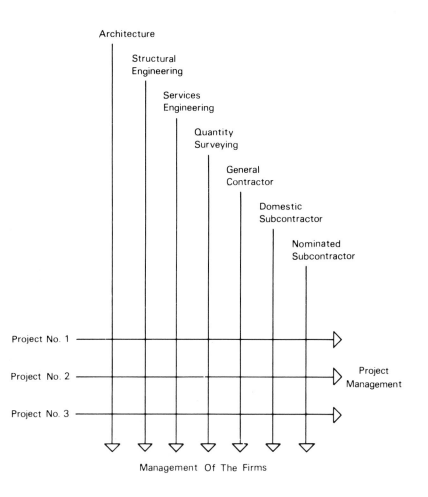

Fig. 1.1   Simplified matrix management structure.

This diagram is greatly simplified because it implies that the three projects are each being undertaken by the same professional practices, general contractor and subcontractors. In practice, of course, this is rarely the case. Normally there will be different mixes of professional practices, general contractors and subcontractors on each project. Even if the private practices are the same, by using competitive tendering it is very unlikely that the general contractor and subcontractors will remain the same.

Construction projects are therefore undertaken by an amalgam of firms, which change from project to project. The firms involved in each project are independent companies, which are organisationally interdependent in terms of the project. This situation creates a potential for conflict between the needs of each firm and of each project. Each firm has objectives which are expressed in terms concerned with the efficiency of the firm, such as:

(a) increasing productivity,
(b) improving service,
(c) maintaining existing clients,
(d) attracting new business.

The major purpose is to improve effectiveness and hence service and profits. Professional practices would claim to be less entrepreneurial than contracting organisations, but nevertheless conflicts between the needs of individual firms and the needs of projects will still arise. For instance, what does a firm do if there is a choice to be made because of limited resources between progressing an urgent matter for an existing client and undertaking a piece of work that could clinch a commission with a new client? Similarly, what would a contractor do if faced with a choice between keeping a piece of equipment on site to be used to keep a project on programme and removing it to another site in order to increase his profit on the second site, knowing that liquidated damages are unlikely to be claimed on the first site?

The objectives of project management, which ideally should also be the objectives of the firms involved in the project are, as has been said, the objectives of the client. These will relate directly to the project and will be:

(a) functional satisfaction,
(b) aesthetic satisfaction,
(c) completion on time,

(d)   completion within budget,

(e)   value for money.

Where, then, does the responsibility lie for ensuring that the project's objectives are met? The professional practices, particularly architects in a conventional arrangement, would say that it rests with them. But who, then, is to resolve the conflicts that may occur in a manner which is to the benefit of the particular project? If the practices are to do it, can they be sufficiently unbiased to resolve conflict to the benefit of the project to the extent to which the client may require?

The matrix structure using independent firms seems to need the responsibility for project management to rest in a firm or individual who is independent of the potential conflicts within the contributing firms. But may not such a firm also be faced with similar conflicts if dealing with a stream of projects?

Ideally it seems that project management should be exercised by the client organisation itself, and this reflects the need for clients to be very close to the organisation and implementation of their projects. However, many clients do not have the expertise to manage their own projects. This, therefore, is the dilemma for clients and for project management. Clients should be concerned to ensure that the design of organisation structures for their projects recognises and seeks to overcome such potential conflicts.

These issues raise the question as to whether the building process is unique. It may not be unique in terms of its organisation problems, but it is perhaps unique in that the problems pervade all levels of construction activity and in many countries are firmly rooted in the historic development of the industry and its professions.

Interestingly, focus on the project management process has emerged from complex projects outside the construction industry, for example in connection with the space programme in the U.S.A. and in other industries facing complex demands that require inputs from a range of independent firms. The situation they are facing has been present in construction certainly since the last century.

It has taken the complexity and constraints of today's world, together with initiatives from outside the industry, to focus attention upon the way projects are managed as a possible means of finding solutions to some of the problems the industry faces. This reflects much of what Marian Bowley[4] deduced about the inertia within the building industry and professions which has stifled innovation.

COMBINATIONS OF CONTRIBUTORS

The possible combinations of practices and contractors are illustrated by the fact that in the U.K. alone there are about 4000 architectural practices and 2800 quantity surveying practices, over 5000 estate surveying practices, more than 35000 general contractors and 50000 subcontractors, plus all the specialist engineering consultancies. Even though many of the organisations are extremely small, the figures illustrate the scale of the industry in the U.K. and give an appreciation of the scale world-wide. In addition there are about 220 local government organisations in the U.K. with chief architects and hence supporting departments, and about 120 with chief estate officers, as well as central government, nationalised industries and industrial and commercial companies with similar groups of specialists, all of which are repeated in some form in many other countries.

With such a large number of firms involved, it is hardly surprising that there is limited opportunity for the same combination of contributors to be engaged on more than one project. Such a lack of consistency of contributors makes it extremely difficult to improve the effectiveness of the project management process. Not only do firms have to get used to each other at both a corporate and individual level, but they are also unlikely to invest much time and money in making the process more effective when they know that any temporary management structure that they establish may only occasionally be used in a similar form again.

ORGANISATION PATTERNS

The major organisation structure referred to so far has been the conventional arrangement of independent professional firms and contractors selected in competition. However, the variation in organisation patterns induced by other types of firm should not be overlooked.

There has been a growth in recent years in interdisciplinary group professional practices and joint ventures for overseas contracts which should overcome some of the problems associated with the variation in professional firms contributing to projects. Similar advantages could also accrue to interdisciplinary local and central government groups but, on the other hand, if a public service department provides only one type of professional service for their project (e.g. architecture) and uses professional firms for other services, the problems of organisation may be even more complex.

Different organisation patterns are also generated by the way in which the general contractor and subcontractors are selected. A range of alternatives is available, for instance design-and-build, two-stage tendering and negotiated contracts. One then has to add to this what is probably the most significant variable: the vast range of client types served by the industry.

VARIETY OF CLIENTS

Clients vary in many ways. Of particular importance is the variety of objectives that clients seek to satisfy. Differences in this respect are particularly marked between private and public sector clients, and overseas and multinational clients may have objectives rarely encountered in home markets.

The variety of objectives is compounded by the range of uncertainty of clients' objectives. The construction industry and its professions have to be skilled at translating such variability in a way which enables them to produce projects that satisfy their clients. They have to deal directly with their clients and in order to do this, and obtain and interpret instructions properly, they need to understand how their clients' organisations operate as the organisation structures used by clients vary considerably to reflect the needs of clients' major activities. As everyone, either individually or corporately, is a potential client for construction work, the construction industry and its professions could be called upon to work with every or any possible organisation configuration. The industry and its professions need to understand how organisations work in order to organise themselves and also to understand how their clients' organisations work, so that they may be in the most advantageous position to interpret and implement their clients' objectives.

The demands that both private and public clients place upon the construction process are frequently complex and uncertain. This simply reflects the complexity and uncertainty of the modern world, as demonstrated by contemporary economic, social and environmental issues. The construction industry and its professions are themselves also subjected directly to such forces.

When establishing temporary management structures for construction projects within such an environment, the industry has available a range of organisational approaches but has tended to adopt a conventional solution. Such a standard answer cannot necessarily be expected to solve problems as complex as these.

The professions and industry should more readily develop approaches to the design of organisation structures that are tailored to satisfying specific client objectives, and take advantage of the range of temporary management structures available.

LIMITATIONS OF THE CONTRIBUTION OF ORGANISATION STRUCTURES

It is important to put the orientation of this book about organisation structures into a broader management context. There are many factors other than organisation structure that have a significant bearing upon the performance of an organisation. However, organisation structure is a particularly important aspect as, if properly designed, it allows the other aspects to function properly.

This is not to say that, if an organisation is inappropriately designed, it will not perform adequately, as people have the ability to construct informal organisation structures that circumvent the formal structure often to the benefit of performance. However, a strong informal structure can work against organisation co-ordination and control. The ideal is when the organisation is sufficiently well designed that it does not generate an informal structure. Such an outcome would mean that the organisation is designed to meet its specific objectives and that the participating members would have confirmed that, in their view, this is in fact the case.

An appropriately designed organisation structure for a project will provide the framework within which the other factors that influence the effectiveness of the project management process have the best chance of maximum performance in the interests of achieving a client's objectives. For the purpose of construction project management, the major internal factors influencing the effectiveness of the management process can be considered to be:

(a) behavioural responses,
(b) techniques and technology,
(c) decision making,
(d) organisation structure.

These aspects are interrelated and interdependent, as illustrated in fig. 1.2.

The project management process is also subject to external influences. These comprise all elements outside the process which, if they change, demand a response from the project management process if it is to remain effective. Examples are economic forces, which may affect the client and modify his objectives for the project, and legal forces, which may require changes to the design, e.g. revised building regulations.

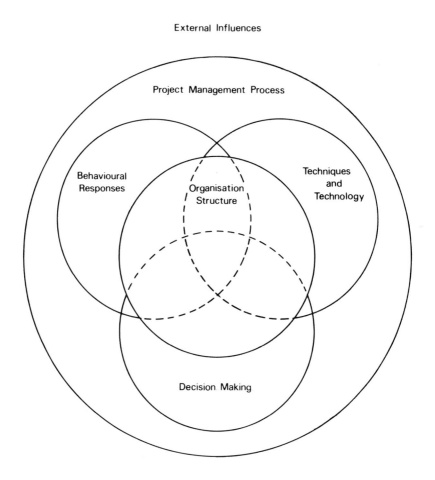

Fig. 1.2   Factors in the project management process.

BEHAVIOURAL RESPONSES

The behavioural factor consists of the characteristics of the individual members of the organisation as reflected in their motivation, reaction to status and role relationships and their personal goals and values. It therefore determines the attitude they have to their work on the project and to the work of others. Attitudes are significantly affected by external influences (e.g. the views of society) in addition to being influenced by the other aspects of the management process. Behavioural responses have particular significance for construction project management because of the sentience of the various professions and skills involved, many of which have strong allegiances and view projects from very different positions, as illustrated in fig. 1.3. It is a factor that can have a significant impact on the effectiveness of the project management process.

TECHNIQUES AND TECHNOLOGY

Techniques and technology are the tools used by the members of the organisation to produce the building or other construction work. The quality of the tools they use is determined by the knowledge the project team have of the techniques and technologies available and their skill in using them. The interdependency of the organisation structure and the techniques and technology used is based upon the need for the organisation to be structured in such a way that the appropriate techniques and technologies are drawn upon and used at the correct time in the process of designing and constructing. As a corollary, the techniques and technologies adopted may demand a certain organisation of the contributors to make their use effective. The techniques employed and the way in which they are put together by the project management process are fundamental to achieving clients' objectives. They encompass evaluation, appraisal and control methods, contractual techniques and approaches to design, as well as the techniques of constructing the project. Particularly important for construction projects is the project information facility employed and how this relates to the organisation structure.

DECISION MAKING

Although the quality of decision making is vital for all organisations, it acquires special status on construction projects. The complexity of projects is reflected by the large number of specialists who contribute to the decision-making process. It is therefore closely related to the organisation structure, which determines how people work

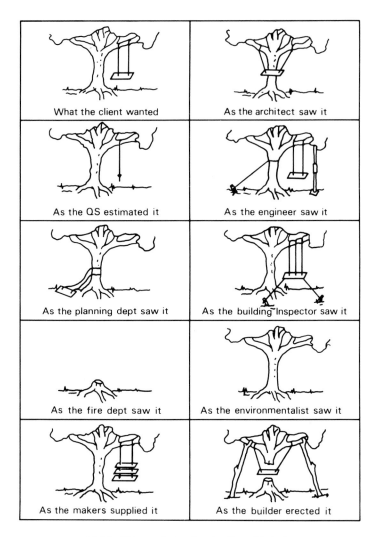

What the client wanted	As the architect saw it
As the QS estimated it	As the engineer saw it
As the planning dept saw it	As the building Inspector saw it
As the fire dept saw it	As the environmentalist saw it
As the makers supplied it	As the builder erected it

(Original idea and sketches by Dave Taylor)

Fig. 1.3 Perspectives of the contributors.

together to produce the output that forms the basis on which decisions are made.

In moving towards the completed building, the process is characterised by a series of 'pinch points' through which it must pass if it is to make progress. At each of the points, a decision has to be made which could include the option to abort the project. The process of making these decisions will be managed by the project management process as a whole and will be based on output generated by the contributors working within the organisation structure using techniques and technologies. The client and managing executive will take many of these decisions based on the advice of the specialist contributors. The significance of decision making is that it should be interrelated with the organisation structure in such a way that advice is received by the decision maker from the appropriate contributors at the appropriate time.

ORGANISATION STRUCTURE

The organisation structure of a particular construction project is a subset of the project's management process. It structures the relationships of the members of the organisation and hence influences their responses to the demands placed on them. It establishes the way in which advice is generated for decision making and the use of techniques and technology in the process. It should be designed to allow these factors to be integrated.

The managing executive of the project should be responsible for designing the organisation structure and then should provide the integrating activities that weld the parts into a unified whole. The managing executive then provides the dynamism required to make the whole process seek to achieve the client's objectives.

LIMITATIONS

This book is primarily concerned with the criteria against which the design of the organisation structure can be judged for particular construction projects. Later in the book, a systems view is developed which cannot ignore the other major factors that influence the effectiveness of the project management process. However, they will be referred to in relation to the design of the organisation structure since the effectiveness of the structure for construction projects will determine to a large degree the effectiveness of the whole process.

REFERENCES

1. Wilson, A.J. (1976) 'Thirteenth Century Project Management'. *Building Technology and Management* Vol. 14 (No. 7).
2. Cleland, D.I. and King, W.R. (1975) *Systems Analysis and Project Management.* 2nd. edn. New York: McGraw-Hill.

3. Likert, R. (1961) *New Patterns of Management.* New York: McGraw-Hill.
4. Bowley, M. (1966) *The British Building Industry.* Cambridge: Cambridge University Press.

2 Evolution of Project Organisation

INTRODUCTION

The way in which construction projects are organised in different countries has evolved from traditions and conventions laid down in each country many years ago. The traditions and conventions of the U.K. have had a particularly wide significance as they have been exported to many parts of the world over the last two centuries. A brief account of project organisation evolution in the U.K. may help to explain the position reached in trying to develop more effective ways of managing construction projects. It will have been paralleled in many other countries.

ORIGINS

The way in which contributors to construction projects organise themselves in the U.K. at the present time has its origins in the Middle Ages, but the original patterns have been influenced significantly by the increasing complexity of the conditions in which building has taken place and by the construction industry's attempts to cope with the prevailing conditions.

The surviving records of building in the Middle Ages are for prestigious structures and mainly show that a master mason was responsible for acquiring and organising labour and material and for the technicalities of construction on the basis of an outline from the client. Alongside master craftsmen there often existed clients' representatives, many of whom did not have practical experience of building but who were among the few people who were literate and numerate. They were expert administrators and went under a variety of titles, such as surveyor, clerk of works and sacrist. The client would pay directly for the labour and material consumed.

This direct method predominated until towards the end of the seventeenth century, although there is evidence as early as the beginning of the sixteenth century of work being let on a contract or 'bargain' basis. This basic pattern probably had many variants as the recorded titles of people are confusing and the relative responsibilities difficult to determine.

The eminence of master masons led to the most eminent being appointed King's Mason with responsibility for oversight of the king's palaces and castles. They also acted as advisers on a number of projects, in a role akin to that of architect in later years.

The relatively stable conditions in which the 'building industry' existed in the medieval period did not create conditions for change in the organisational pattern of building work until demand for building began to rise in the sixteenth century, when the distinctive role of the architect began to emerge and more work began to be awarded on a contract or 'bargain' basis. Engineers were more concerned with mechanical devices for military purposes than with buildings, but through their work on fortifications and castles their influence on buildings began to be felt although master craftsmen developed their own empirical engineering and jealously guarded this knowledge.

The period from the sixteenth century to the Industrial Revolution saw many changes, which had profound effects on the organisation of building projects. England had become a principal trading country of the world and travel had awakened interest in the buildings of ancient Greece and Rome, leading to a demand for such designs. This led to the clearer identification of the role of the architect, and the associated complexity resulted in an increasing tendency to let building work on a contract basis, although 'architects' also often acted as developers. Further impetus to change was created by the Great Fire of London, which led to the 'measure and value' method of settling payments and the employment of separate measurers. There still appears to have been little application of formal engineering to building, although some road and bridge building took place.

The great surge in the demand placed upon the construction industry was generated by the Industrial Revolution. The accompanying prosperity created demands for housing, to accommodate both workers and owners, and for buildings for the new industries. The demand for improved transportation led to the development of new engineering and building techniques, and to further industrialisation and demand for buildings. In response to such demands, new materials were being developed, which allowed new building techniques to be devised.

These activities created a concentration upon the specialist skills of the members of the building industry. The importance of the engineer emerged; there was the further separation of the architect and builder as specialists; quantity surveying skills were more firmly identified; and engineering was subdivided into civil, mechanical and electrical skills. However, this was an incremental process and specialists often acted in dual capacities.

The new complexity of the conditions within which construction work was executed, with greater emphasis on economy, value and prestige, the complexity of new building materials and technologies and the developing skills of the building industry specialists themselves, created the need for greater specialisation among them. These pressures led to the establishment of societies for the discussion of common problems. Architectural clubs were formed in 1791, but clubs for civil engineers had been set up as early as 1771. In 1834 clubs were established for surveyors and for builders. Subsequently, to protect themselves from economic pressures on the one hand and from the unscrupulous on the other, the clubs developed, in the nineteenth century, into professional institutions as the means of defining their position and creating their public image through the acquisition of royal patronage. This further emphasised the separation of the skills associated with construction and so reinforced allegiance to specialist skills rather than the industry as a whole, and created the basis from which today's conventional organisational structure for construction projects has grown.

The period from the late nineteenth century to the First World War saw a continuing rapid increase in the growth of the building industry. This was accompanied by the rise of the general builder for both speculative and contract work, and the parallel emergence of specialist craft firms. This occurred in response to the need for organising ability and financial strengths required for the process of urbanisation and industrialisation.

The architectural profession was moulded on the social and aesthetic pattern of the eighteenth century, when architecture was considered one of the arts with the actual construction of the building being secondary. By the late nineteenth century, the idea that there should be any connection between architects and the mass of industrial buildings and working class housing seems to have been generally disregarded. Architects were, by then, concerned primarily with prestigious buildings. These attitudes were reflected in the 1887 supplementary charter of the Royal Institute of British Architects, which laid down that no member of the Institute could hold a profit-making position in the building industry and retain his membership.

This separation of architects and builders was accompanied by further separation of architects and engineers. The development of industrialisation and the position adopted by architects decreed that industrial building was the province of engineers but, at the same time, engineers were commonly employed to advise on the structure of architect-designed buildings. Hence, architects were technically dependent upon engineers, but engineers were not dependent upon architects. Significantly, engineers did not exclude themselves from being principals of engineering or building firms. Further separation occurred when, in 1907, the Royal Institution of Chartered Surveyors instituted the Contractors' Rule, which prohibited its members from being employed by construction firms.

Bowley[1] describes the pattern that emerged as 'the system' and believes that it had acquired a strong flavour of social class distinctions, architects being the elite. Engineers were associated with trade and industry, surveyors were on the next rung of the social hierarchy and builders were regarded as being 'in trade'. She believes that, as a result, aesthetic and technical innovations in the late nineteenth and early twentieth centuries were completely out of step with each other, which inhibited the development of the major technical innovations of steel-framed and reinforced concrete structures *vis à vis* other countries and created a conservatism in the construction professions.

Building activity between the First and Second World Wars was much greater than before 1914. However, there were no important changes in the way in which the design and production of buildings were organised, although the efficiency of site operations was enhanced, particularly through mechanisation. The period was one of consolidation of the main professions through the establishment of professional qualifications tested by examination and of codes of conduct, which raised their status and reinforced adherence to the established pattern of project organisation.

The lack of innovation in building in Britain in this period was brought about primarily as a result of the lack of a built-in mechanism in the organisation of design and construction that could create the necessary stimulus. The innovations that did take place tended to be outside the industry, particularly in the organisation of the building materials industry and in the materials themselves. In addition, there was great concern with housing needs and the switch from commercial speculative development to public development reinforced the prevailing pattern of organisation as this work also used the same structures. The pattern of organisation of design and construction does not appear to have been fundamentally questioned during this period, as reflected in the list of official government publications, none of which were concerned with organisation but which concentrated mainly on materials and housing.

Present-day organisation arrangements for building projects and attitudes to innovations within the industry still reflect, to a degree, the conservatism generated by patterns laid down before the Second World War. However, there are indications, following a succession of official reports on these topics, that the professions and industry are responding to the demands of an environment far more complex than that in which the patterns were originally established. The dramatic developments in transportation, communications, health care, manufacturing technologies and the associated economic, social and technological order have been important forces for change in the construction industry. One response has been the abandonment of the Contractors' Rule by the R.I.C.S. and the recent merger with the I.Q.S.

A PERSPECTIVE OF CONTEMPORARY INFLUENCES

THE SECOND WORLD WAR AND POST-WAR ACTIVITY

The impetus to innovation provided by the Second World War was dramatic and focussed upon the need for economy in labour and reduction in the use of materials in short supply. This need was demonstrated by the rapid adoption of prestressed concrete, pre-fabricated buildings and the tendency to replace steel with reinforced concrete. Wartime also generated the first governmental enquiry[2] directly concerned with the organisation of building work, which was the forerunner of reports that questioned the suitability and efficiency of the prevailing organisation of the construction process. Nevertheless, this report accepted the established patterns and concerned itself, primarily, with tendering methods and arrangements for subcontractors.

Following the Second World War, the demands placed upon the

building industry rapidly increased in complexity. The pressures created by the need for rebuilding in the aftermath of war were followed by an acceleration in complexity of demand through the development of the Welfare State, which required new and more advanced buildings. Also, the increased sophistication of industry required increasingly sophisticated buildings and there arose the need to redevelop cities to cope with a more technological age. One of the driving forces behind these demands was the increase in the relative importance of government-sponsored buildings and the consequently greater involvement of government in building. The tendency to build larger production units, arising from the development of large-scale organisations in industry, was another important force.

In spite of the substantial changes in demand placed upon the industry, the pattern of organisation of projects remained largely unaltered. Increased government sponsorship of building projects served to reinforce allegiance to the traditional pattern by the need for public accountability, which was seen to be satisfied by competitive tendering on finished designs. Nevertheless, there were some innovations in organisation patterns through the use of negotiated tenders and 'design-and-build', but the resistance to change of the established pattern is illustrated by the reluctance of public authorities to adopt selective, as opposed to open, tendering even though this had been strongly recommended in the Simon Report[2] of 1944 and again in the Phillips Report[3] of 1950. Other developments were concerned with improving the effectiveness of site operations, particularly through prefabrication and in-house construction.

However, the need for greater co-operation began to be recognised following the Phillips Report, which commented upon the ease with which variations could be introduced during construction, the problems created by drawings issued late, the extensive use of nominated subcontractors and the desirability of establishing a common basic education for all those involved in the design of buildings and their production.

Increasingly, discussion centred upon the need for greater co-operation between all parties to the construction process. This was further stimulated by the greater need for engineers to be involved in the more complicated buildings being demanded, the necessity for reliable cost control and an increase in the number of large building firms.

The difficulties of the traditional pattern of organisation in coping with the demands of modern construction, which were evident between the wars, were greatly intensified after the Second World War, but the greater spirit of co-operation within the industry that had begun to emerge took place against the backcloth of the existing traditions and was not concerned with a fundamental reappraisal of the structure that had been established. This situation was reflected in the next major official enquiry, the Emmerson Report[4] in 1962, which reiterated the findings of the previous two post-war reports regarding the need to improve co-ordination of the members of the building team.

THE SIGNIFICANT REPORTS OF THE 1960s
Although it was also concerned with supply and demand in the building industry, standards of training, research and technical information, the Emmerson Report is particularly significant for its observations on relationships within the construction professions and industry, and with clients, and in connection with the placing and management of contracts. It identified a common criticism of the construction process as the lack of liaison between architects and the other professions and contractors, and between them and clients. It commented, 'In no other important industry is the responsibility for design so far removed from the responsibility for production.' The report pointed out that although a common course of initial study for designers and producers of buildings had been recommended in 1950, no practical steps had been taken by 1962. Emmerson came to the conclusion that there was still a general failure to adopt enlightened methods of tendering in spite of the recommendations of earlier reports. His recommendations in this respect led directly to the establishment of the Banwell Committee[5] later in 1962, to consider these issues in more detail.

Of the official reports, the Banwell Report, published in 1964, and its review 'Action on the Banwell Report'[6] in 1967 had a significant impact upon the building industry and its professions. A particular concern of the report was the unnecessarily restricted and inefficient practices of the professions, leading to over-compartmentalisation and the failure of the industry and its professions to think and act together. The 1967 review found some progress on preplanning projects but noted that the professions had done little to 'de-restrict' their practices. The review was encouraged by the increase in selective tendering and urged further consideration of serial and negotiated tendering.

The Emmerson and Banwell Reports brought into sharp focus the need to reform the approach to the organisation of construction projects. They were accompanied by other reports making similar points. At the time, construction project management was seen to be a passive procedural activity but the movement towards a more dynamic integrated approach was being suggested by Higgins and Jessop[7] in a pilot study sponsored by the National Joint Consultative Committee of Architects, Quantity Surveyors and Builders. They clearly identified that the problems of communication in the building industry were created to a large extent by attitudes and perceptions about the values of contributors to the building process. They were probably the first to suggest that overall co-ordination of design and construction should be exercised by a single person (or group). Concurrently, a review of the construction industry by the National Economic Development Council[8] was calling for improvement in the management of the construction process, and the co-ordination of activities of the members of the construction team and the administrative framework within which they were working. A rather rhetorical report[9] by the Institute of Economic Affairs was also condemning the restrictive practices of the professions.

This spate of activity and concern with the performance and organisation of the industry and its professions marked the beginning of a self-examination. It was induced, to a large degree, by external pressures that reflected the greater complexity of the influences at work upon the industry and its clients. The economic expansion of the early 1960s and rapidly developing technology and changing social attitudes were manifested in demands for more complex and sophisticated buildings and a more economic utilisation of resources. These forces were transmitted to the industry through its clients and also directly affected its techniques and attitudes, but such self-examination was likely to be slow when undertaken in the presence of the polarisation of skills and attitudes inherent in the professional structure that had emerged over the preceding century.

The reorientation of management studies of the construction process that had begun to take place is well illustrated by the Building Research Station's report[10] in 1968. This identified the fact that up to that date most of the work of the B.R.S. had been concerned with the management of building sites and building firms but noted that future work would be concerned more with the management of the total building process.

THE PROJECT MANAGER AND OTHER ORGANISATION INITIATIVES
During the 1960s and subsequently, progress has been made in developing collaborative work and skills, and in instituting procedures that provide a variety of organisational patterns, particularly in connection with the introduction of the contractor at various stages of the design process. However, there was still a need in official reports in 1975, 1976 and 1978 (see references 11 to 13) to stress that more attention should be paid to structuring and managing project organisations to create conditions for co-operation between contributors. Each of these reports recognised the distinctive nature of the project management process and the role of the project manager, and reflected the changes in attitudes and views expressed since the mid-1960s. They arose from the distillation of the professions' and industry's experience of working with novel forms of organisation. The 1976 report recognised the need for further study which would analyse existing patterns in the use of alternative methods of organisation of the design and construction process.

The external pressures that have caused the professions to reconsider organisational arrangements for projects have been accompanied by challenges from the Monopolies and Mergers Commission in relation to their codes of conduct and fee scales. Further pressure has been brought to bear through the definition and development of project management concepts and applications in other industries and the recognition by project management theorists that the concepts and techniques are applicable to construction. The professions' and industry's response to these influences reflects the manner in which the traditional structures emerged. Each sector has pursued its own approach to project management while recognising rather reluctantly that the role of project manager was not the right of any one profession.

A reflection of the uncoordinated empirical evolution of project management as an activity separated from design skills is given by the number of definitions that have emerged in recent years. The Chartered Institute of Building's paper[14] identifies thirteen definitions. It comments that the confusion of terminology and usage is unsatisfactory, and proposes a further definition! It is, perhaps, to be expected that those writing on such an important emerging idea, which is contrary to their traditional backgrounds, should seek to express their ideas in their own words. However, this results in a range of definitions that tend to reflect the particular background and experience of the writer rather than a generalised definition of the concept.

The empirical nature of publications on project management is reflected in their emphasis on defining the jobs to be done by a project manager at various stages of a particular project rather than identifying the concept and process of project management. Nevertheless, such publications have been useful in emphasising the patterns that can be adopted with advantage to the client.

Against this background of pressure for change in organisational approaches there have been a number of project-based initiatives. The project manager idea is only one rather ill-defined idea which has been used to cover a range of organisational patterns. Others include *management contracting,* which is designed to introduce construction skills into the design stage but which does not necessarily overcome the problems of integration as polarisation of professional attitudes is not directly affected; *research into site management* (R.S.M.), developed by Nottinghamshire County Council, which requires the design team to be directly involved in the construction process; and *alternative methods of management* (A.M.M.), a concept which also requires the design team to be involved in the organisation of the actual construction process through the integration of sub-contracts. Both R.S.M. and A.M.M. demand that the design team be on site for the majority of a project's construction stage. These approaches are directly concerned with integrating the design and construction activities while maintaining the client's independent professional advisers. They take a positive approach to overcoming differentiation of the skills involved in construction projects. Other techniques, which do not take such a positive stance but seek to overcome the same problem, are *design and construct contracts* and *negotiated contracts.*

Although useful for learning from the experience of others, such developments do not provide a generalised conceptual framework that allows identification of the features of significance in the construction process as a basis for designing organisation structures that take account of them. A conceptual framework is now needed that allows project management functions to be identified so as to reflect the demands of different projects and resolve the differences that appear to exist when identifying functions from an empirical base.

Techniques for project control (e.g. critical path networks, discounted cash flow) have been available for some time, but their rate of application has been variable depending upon the inclination of the team leader who traditionally has been the architect. Indeed, project management is sometimes seen as a collection of techniques rather than the framework in which they are applied. The British Standards Committee on Project Management changed the title of its guide from *Guide to Project Management* to *Guide to the Use of Network Techniques in Project Management* to avoid such misunderstanding. A significant amount of research has been undertaken on industry-wide information systems and data co-ordination and the resultant computer applications. However, their implementation on an industry-wide basis, which should significantly increase the industry's efficiency, has been inhibited by the lack of an hospitable framework of project organisation. In 1970, it was said[15] that the problems of development and implementation of information systems would not be finally resolved until a widespread reorientation in the thinking habits of professionals had taken place.

RELEVANCE OF SYSTEMS THEORY

There have been some valuable isolated initiatives in response to the pleas of the successive official reports for greater co-ordination, but there remains a resistance to change which reflects the attitudes and loyalties of those concerned. Against such a background, any progress will have to be incremental. However, an equally significant inhibition to progress is the lack of a fundamental framework of organisational theory relating to construction projects against which experience of the various organisational initiatives can be measured and compared.

Systems theory may provide the opportunity to develop such a framework. *General systems theory* (G.S.T.)[16] originated in the biological sciences, but its originator, Von Bertalanffy, has acknowledged its general applicability, which he considers encompasses business organisations. It has been usefully applied to organisational problems in industries other than the construction industry.

The attraction of systems theory as a medium for identifying a conceptual framework for the management of the construction process lies in the basic premise that a system is an organised or complex whole: an assemblage or combination of things or parts forming a complex or unitary whole, which is greater than the simple sum of the parts. The systems approach stresses the contribution of the interrelationships of the parts of the system and the system's adaptation to its environment in achieving its objective. The value of the application of systems concepts to the organisation design of the construction process has been suggested by systems experts and applications have been made by Morris, Napier and Handler.

Peter Morris[17] developed an approach to studying integration of the participants at the design-construction interface of construction projects. The work compared six projects with different stages of contractor appointment to the project team. He took a rather narrow view of the construction process by focussing attention solely on the design-construction interface. The management of a project is concerned with the total design and construction process and requires a consideration of all the interfaces in the total process. Nevertheless, Morris's work supported the systems approach in that he found that organisation theory, especially when employed in the context of a systems framework, could be used to describe and explain the nature of the management process of construction projects.

A further application of the systems concept was made in Sweden by Napier.[18] In this work he attempted to gain an understanding of the problems of the Swedish building industry as a whole as a basis for the design of systems for the future. He drew almost exclusively upon the work of the Tavistock Institute and concluded that his theoretical model seemed to function well as an instrument for interpretation. By considering the building industry as a system with a number of sub-systems, and by studying these systems in their environment, it has been possible for him to obtain a realistic picture of the industry and the causes of its major problems.

Handler[19] was principally concerned with the building as a system. This concept was developed by reference to general systems theory, by drawing an analogy between a living organism and a building. The concept of a building as a system was transferred to the need for architects to design buildings from this concept. Handler's work was basically an abstraction of the manner in which architects should work and think rather than how the building process should be organised, although he recognised in passing the need for a structure to integrate the work of specialists and the value of the systems concept in its achievement.

These studies illustrate the potential for the application of systems theory to the building process. Each study has taken a different perspective, but has employed the same basic concepts. The fundamental premiss of systems theory stresses interrelationships and is as concerned with the links between the parts of the system as with the parts themselves. The problem of how to make the links work effectively is essentially the problem of project management. In order to apply these ideas to the construction process to the greatest benefit, it is necessary to take as broad a perspective of the process as possible from conception of the project to completion and even beyond.

REFERENCES

1. Bowley, M. (1966) *The British Building Industry*. Cambridge: Cambridge University Press.
2. *Report on the Management and Planning of Contracts (The Simon Report)* (1944). London: H.M.S.O.
3. *Report of the Working Party on the Building Industry (The Phillips Report)* (1950). London: H.M.S.O.
4. *Survey of the Problems before the Construction Industries (The Emmerson Report)* (1962). London: H.M.S.O.
5. *The Placing and Management of Contracts for Building and Civil Engineering Works (The Banwell Report)* (1964). London: H.M.S.O.
6. *A Survey of the Implementation of the Recommendations of the Committee under the Chairmanship of Sir Harold Banwell on the Placing and Management of Contracts for Building and Civil Engineering Works (Action on the Banwell Report)* (1967). London: H.M.S.O.
7. Higgins, G. and Jessop, N. (1965) *Communication in the Building Industry*. London: Tavistock Publications.
8. National Economic Development Council (1964) *The Construction Industry*. London: National Economic Development Office, H.M.S.O.
9. Knox, F. and Hennesey, J. (1966) *Restrictive Practices in the Building Industry*. London: Institute of Economic Affairs.
10. Bishop, D. (1968) *The Background to Management Studies by the B.R.S.* London: Building Research Station Current Paper 60/68.
11. National Economic Development Council (1976) *The Public Client and the Construction Industries*. London: National Economic Development Office, H.M.S.O.
12. National Economic Development Council (1976) *The Professions in the Construction Industries*. London: National Economic Development Office, H.M.S.O.
13. National Economic Development Council (1978) *Construction for Industrial Recovery*. London: National Economic Development Office, H.M.S.O.

14. *Project Management in Building, Occasional Paper No. 20* (1979). Ascot: the Chartered Institute of Building.
15. Gray, M. (Sept. 1970) 'Perspectives in the British Information Scene'. *Built Environment.*
16. Von Bertalanffy, L. (1969) *General Systems Theory: Essays on its Foundation and Development.* New York: Braziller.
17. Morris, P.W.G. (1972) *A Study of Selected Building Projects in the Context of Theories of Organisation.* Ph.D. Thesis, University of Manchester, Institute of Science and Technology.
18. Napier, J.A. (1970) *A Systems Approach to the Swedish Building Industry.* Stockholm: the National Swedish Institute for Building.
19. Handler, A.B. (1970) *Systems Approach to Architecture.* Amsterdam: Elsevier.

3 Systems Thinking and Construction Project Organisation

INTRODUCTION

The aim of this chapter is to introduce some of the major ideas of systems theory and illustrate their application to the construction process. As a result it should be possible to judge whether the systems approach is useful for gaining a better understanding of the process. The approach is essentially a way of thinking about complex processes so that the interrelationships of the parts and their influence upon the effectiveness of the total process can be better understood, analysed and improved.

OPEN AND CLOSED SYSTEMS

The appeal of the systems approach to the study of construction project organisations arises from its focus on how the parts of a process are dependent upon each other, as illustrated by the following definition of a system:

> Any entity, conceptual or physical, which consists of interdependent parts. Each of a system's elements is connected to every other element, directly or indirectly, and no sub-set of elements is unrelated to any other sub-set.[1]

It is clearly the case that the success of the construction process depends to a large extent upon the way in which the architect, engineer, quantity surveyor, contractors and others work together. It depends upon them perceiving the same objectives for the project and recognising that what each of them achieves depends upon what the others do. With this view they should be able to stand above the particular interests of their own contribution and see the problem posed by the project as a whole. The advent of the project manager has, to a large degree, come about as a result of the inability of the contributors to consistently achieve this, and in response to the consequent need for someone who will concentrate solely upon integrating the various contributors in the interests of the client.

To understand how the building process operates as a system it is necessary to understand the distinction between closed and open systems. A *closed system* is one that does not respond to events and occurrences outside the system. It cannot adapt to changes and is therefore predictable. Machines can be considered to be closed systems in that the parts are selected to perform specific functions in a given set of conditions to produce a predetermined output. If there are changes in the conditions for which the machine was designed, the machine will not adapt to them. For example, a washing machine will not work if overloaded, a motor car will not work properly on dirty petrol.

On the other hand, an *open system* adapts to events and occurrences outside the system. These events and occurrences take place in what is known as the system's environment. This has been defined as a set of elements and their relative properties, which elements are not a part of the system, but a change in any of which can produce a change in the state of the system.[2] An open system has a permeable boundary and there is import and export between an open system and its environment. It is therefore influencing and being influenced by its environment. An open system is dynamic and adapts to its environment by changing its structure and processes. Although stable, it is always changing and evolving and presents differences over time and in changing circumstances. A living organism is an open system and business organisations are analysed as open systems.

However, it is not as clear cut as the closed-open dichotomy implies: there is a range of other classifications. For example, a central heating system and the human body, both of which adapt themselves to changes in the temperature of their environment by internal adjustment so that they remain static, are referred to as homeostatic systems. Also, Child[3] has described a system that exists in a protected environment in which it defends itself from having to adapt fully to its environment. Therefore the system is not fully open.

Business organisations could never have existed as closed systems. Similarly, the construction process has always been an open system. Potential clients exist in the environment of the construction process system and the system must adapt to them. It imports ideas, energy, materials, information, etc. from its environment and transforms them into its output, which is the finished construction. This is then exported to the environment, which is itself influenced by the use to which the completed project is put and by the fact that the construction is an addition to the nation's fixed capital. The process is illustrated in fig. 3.1.

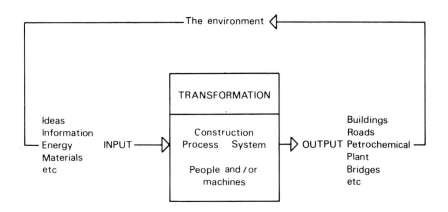

Fig. 3.1   The construction process as an input-output model.

Recognising the construction process as an open system means that the functions upon which the project management process should focus can be summarised as:

(a) identifying, communicating and adapting the system's objectives;
(b) ensuring that the parts of the system are working effectively;
(c) ensuring that appropriate connections are established between the parts;
(d) activating the system so that the connections that have been established work effectively;
(e) relating the total system to its environment and adapting the system as required in response to changes in its environment.

In practical terms the project manager will be concerned particularly with anticipating the chain reactions of decisions and developments that occur on the project. For example, as a result of an upturn in business, the client may decide at a late stage in the design of a project to be submitted for competitive tender that he needs substantially more floor area in his factory. This decision has to be appraised in terms of its effect on the project cost, completion time and functional efficiency, and evaluated against alternatives such as providing the additional area in a different form, e.g. leased accommodation, or by a different method, e.g. a negotiated contract for the additional area. This will require interaction between all the contributors to the project, the complexity of which will depend upon the actual stage of development of the project. The final decision will need to be taken solely in terms of the client's objectives in relation to his revised requirements. For example, completion time not only means additional construction time but also the additional time required by the consultants and the effect this may have on construction completion, particularly if this may mean 'hidden delays' to construction completion because of drawings being issued late or incomplete. The relationship between cost and completion time would also need to be appraised. All of these factors would require interaction between the contributors so that the priority of the competing demands would be resolved in the client's interest. The project manager needs to be able to anticipate the interconnectedness generated by such decisions and to manage the system with respect to them.

TRADITIONAL MANAGEMENT AND THE SYSTEMS APPROACH

TRADITIONAL APPROACHES

Traditionally, qualifying courses for prospective members of the professions associated with construction have not generally included management subjects. Those for prospective members of construction firms may have contained some management but this has tended to concentrate rather narrowly upon the management of the construction firm and of projects only so far as it affected the firm. Consequently, what little management education has been acquired has come from post-qualification courses and *ad hoc* reading. The result has been erratic levels of knowledge of management fundamentals, the management abilities of the professions and industry mainly having been acquired through experience of managing in the real world. Although such experience is vital, its value is reduced if it cannot be gained within a conceptual framework of management theory. The *ad hoc* acquisition of theory has meant that generally most professionals' and industrialists' knowledge relates to the traditional management concepts.

Traditional management 'theory' had a fixed view of management. It evolved around 'principles', which were held to be universal truths about how sound management should be undertaken. The principles were considered to be the only way to manage business activities or processes, irrespective of the external conditions in which they were carried out. Many of the earlier concepts in the social sciences and in organisation theory were therefore closed-system views because they considered the system under study as self-contained. They concentrated only upon the internal operation of the organisation and adopted highly structured approaches.

What is referred to as the classical approach to the design of organisation structures originated from the schools of Fayol, Urwick, Taylor and their contemporaries and successors in the early twentieth century. Their 'principles of management' were concerned with such things as pyramidal structure, unity of command, line and staff, the scalar chain, and span of control. The primary element was the bureaucratic form, with its pyramidal organisation structure and the idea that authority is delegated downwards. Division of labour was advocated so that the sub-goals of the various units would add up to the overall organisational goals, and co-ordination would be handled through the management hierarchy. It may be that the construction professions recognised through their experience that such approaches were not really appropriate to the management problem of construction projects and for this reason did not fully develop management in their training at an earlier date.

This traditional approach to organisation and management was essentially rigid and stemmed from military and church models. It did not make explicit the effects of the human component and external influences on the organisation. Serious study of people in organisations did not begin until it was explicitly recognised that informal organisations existed in parallel with formal organisations. Recognition of informal organisation structures alongside the formal and the shortcomings of organisational theory saw the emergence of the behavioural and social system schools, which believed that the study of management should be centred on interpersonal relations or that it should be seen as a social system. However, questions were raised as to whether the field of human behaviour is equivalent to the field of management, as the nature of the activities of organisations makes this approach impracticable.

Between the traditional and social systems schools are a range of opinions, which are well analysed by Koontz.[4] The major criticism now levelled at these schools of management thought is that they were offered as the one best way to organise. Subsequent organisation structure thinking denies such an assumption, but believes that each school has something to offer within a systems framework.

THE SYSTEMS APPROACH

General systems theory was developing alongside the schools of management thought and it had an attraction for management thinking as it presented an opportunity to converge the strands of thought into an acceptable and theoretically sound framework with less rigidity and more recognition of interdependency in organisations than the traditional 'principles' imply.

The systems approach reflects the scale of interdependency created by the nature of the activities to be undertaken (e.g. the design and construction of a building) and the effects upon the activities of environmental influences. It therefore discounts rigid approaches that propose one method for all circumstances. This is not to say that the systems approach discounts as irrelevant the ideas of traditional management and the behavioural schools, but rather that it provides a framework for understanding and analysing organisations through their internal and external relationships, which places into context the earlier views of organisations. For example, the behaviour of individuals within an organisation remains important but it is more easily understood and relevant if it is seen within the context of the relationships demanded by the activities being undertaken and the environment within which they take place.

CONTINGENCY THEORY

Lawrence and Lorsch's major study[5] led to the contingency theory of organisation design, which states that there is no one best way to organise but rather that organisation is a function of the nature of the task to be carried out and its environment. It encompasses many recent applications of systems ideas to organisations. Lawrence and Lorsch found that different environments, which generate different levels of uncertainty, require varying degrees of separation (differentiation) of organisation units (e.g. architect, engineer, contractor) and hence they require different degrees of integration.

The extent of differentiation within an organisation depends upon the uncertainty and diversity of the environment and the effect this has on the way the task has to be organised and managed. Lawrence and Lorsch state that they found that the amount of differentiation in the effective organisation was consistent with the environmental demand for the interdependence of the parts of the organisation. In developing their contingency theory they state that this starting model is complicated as soon as we move to a complex, multi-unit organisation, in which each unit strives to cope with different parts of the environment. For example, a construction project that is carried out in conditions of uncertainty and is technologically complex requires a wide range of specialist skills, which are closely dependent upon each other, in achieving a successful outcome. As soon as this happens, it introduces the complication of integrating the work of different units. Lawrence and Lorsch see the existence of an integrating unit and conflict-resolution practices as contributing to the quality of integration and in turn to overall performance. In recent years this unit has come to be represented on construction projects by project managers.

A number of other significant research studies led up to the contingency theory. One, by Burns and Stalker,[6] analysed firms in the electronics industry and identified two patterns of organisation and management. The one they termed 'mechanistic' was similar to the classical model referred to earlier. The other, termed 'organic', had a participative character. These classifications corresponded closely to the two types of manager described by McGregor[7] prior to the widespread application of systems thinking to organisations. McGregor provided a vivid contrast between his Theory X and Theory Y. To summarise, Theory X proposed that the average human being has an inherent dislike of work and will avoid it if he can and therefore has to be threatened and controlled to make him work. If workers do not co-operate with the manager, it is because of their inherent attitudes, not because of a lack of ability on the part of the manager. Theory Y, on the other hand, believes that to the human being work is as natural as play or rest and the responsibility for motivation and the employees' attitude to work lies with the manager's skills in handling people. As with the 'mechanistic' and 'organic' structures, Theory X and Theory Y lie at the extremes of a spectrum which illustrates the range of approaches possible. Burns and Stalker did not suggest that either was superior to the other. They concluded that, when taken in context with the task and environment being considered, one pattern will be more appropriate for the specific tasks and environment in question.

The contingency theory is a succinct summary of a great deal of the detailed work that went before it. It is perhaps a reflection of the management discipline's apparent need to sum up a complex situation in just a few words. Child[3] is critical of the contingency theory on these grounds and believes that it has not in the main recognised the organisation design difficulties which may result from the presence of multiple contingencies. He is concerned at the situation in which a configuration of different contingencies is found which are conflicting in terms of organisation design. For instance, a construction project may demand a relatively bureaucratic organisation structure to ensure accountability, but at the same time require a more loosely structured organisation to more readily allow innovation to take place. Child also questions the cost effectiveness of the additional integrating mechanisms required, as he is not convinced that there is evidence that they improve performance.

Nevertheless, even allowing for such criticisms, the systems approach as summarised in the contingency theory provides a framework for thinking about the design of construction project organisations and for analysing them, so that the effect of organisation structure on the outcome of projects can be better understood.

SYSTEMS CONCEPTS

It is worth while to examine the relevance of the major systems concepts to the construction process to see if they can be used to give a better understanding of construction project management. Embedded in the systems approach are a number of common characteristics of systems which, although couched in systems terminology, can be interpreted in terms of the construction process. The universality of the systems approach is demonstrated by the way in which people from diverse industries have found the concepts acceptable and useful when they have worked them through in their own terms.

OBJECTIVE

A system has an objective. The objective should be stated as clearly as possible and developed as further information becomes available. The manager of an organisation must ensure that all members of the organisation are aiming for the same objective, and must attempt to resolve conflicts where they occur. Many business organisations find it difficult to identify their objectives explicitly but it is an important task of the manager to identify as clearly as possible the objectives of the organisation, communicate it to the members and gain their acceptance. If the objective is unacceptable to members, it will be difficult, if not impossible, to avoid conflict, which is damaging to the performance of the organisation.

At first sight the objective of a construction project management system does not seem to be too difficult to visualise and in some ways it is probably easier to establish than for many business organisations. The system's objective is typified by the 'client's brief', in which the client states what he expects from the finished project. However, many clients' briefs are unsatisfactory. Often the client's requirements for cost and time for completion are not stated clearly or are incompatible, and sometimes the functional and aesthetic needs of the building are not fully or properly established. This may be caused by uncertainty created by the conditions in the project's environment, in which case the system has to respond by attempting to find ways of coping with uncertainty. It may be through lack of skill or attention in developing the brief, in which case the project management process has been deficient. In either case, it is of paramount importance that the state of development of the objective be known and understood by all the contributors to the project. In the former case, they will be aware of the degree of uncertainty inherent in the objective and should adopt approaches and techniques that can best allow for this. In the latter case they should be allowed to respond to the brief in order that they can contribute to identifying and rectifying deficiencies, so that they work towards an objective which they believe will satisfy the client.

Although the system's objective may be relatively easy to perceive, it may be difficult to articulate. The chances of conflicting objectives arising on construction projects are quite high, as a result of most projects being developed by a group of independent firms and professions. The objective of a firm may conflict with the objective of the project team, and the sentience of the different contributors may lead to conflicting interpretations of the project's objectives. The manager of the project will therefore have to set the project's objectives. He must ensure that they are accepted, understood and interpreted consistently by the contributors and must attempt to resolve any conflicts as they arise.

However, systems theory has rather more to say about objectives than this rather simple view. For instance, it considers long-term and shorter-term objectives, the latter often referred to as the goal and the former the objective, but these ideas are often more useful to an analysis of the firm rather than of the project management process. Systems theory also recognises the equifinality of open systems. This means that open systems can reach the same objective from different initial conditions and by a variety of paths. The project manager can therefore use a variety of inputs in different arrangements in the organisation of construction projects and can transfer these in various ways to achieve a satisfactory output. Thus the project management function is not necessarily to identify a rigid approach to achieving the system's objectives but is to have available a variety of approaches. This view can be extended further. Not only does an open system not adopt a rigid approach; it does not necessarily seek a rigid solution, but has a variety of satisfactory solutions which may meet its objectives.

In terms of construction project management, this concept re-minds us that the satisfaction of the objectives of the client does not have to be achieved by the construction of a project. The client has a variety of solutions open to him. He may decide that rather than building he may be able to take over another company in order to achieve his objective, or he may choose to reorganise his own activities to achieve what he requires. Even if it is decided that a building is necessary, the project manager can achieve this for the client in a number of ways, each requiring different inputs and achieving the same or different outcomes, all of which may satisfy the client's objectives. If, for example, the project manager satisfies the client by leasing an existing building, the project manager will use different inputs than if a new building were constructed. If the decision is to construct a new building, there are various arrange-ments that can be used to provide it, e.g. conventional arrangements, design-and-build, etc. This leads to the recognition that the client is part of the project management system or, more constructively, that the construction project management system is temporarily a sub-system of the client's organisation system for the duration of the project.

ENVIRONMENT

A system's environment consists of all elements outside the system that can affect the system's state, as defined earlier. This means that environments can be very complex, yet it is not possible to understand an organisation as a system without a constant study of the forces that impinge upon it. One of the major jobs of the manager of a construction project is to relate that project to its environment. The manager should not be concerned only with the internal regulation of the system. As the system has to respond to changes in its environment, the project manager must be able to detect and analyse such changes if he is to adapt the internal organisation of the system in response to them. Project managers will be closely involved with issues and problems within the project system but their actions should be orientated to their understanding of the external influences acting upon the project organisation.

The process of providing a project is a response to the actions of the environment. The environment acts in two ways upon the process: indirectly upon the activities of the client of an individual project and directly upon the process itself. At its root it is the action of forces in the environment of the client's organisation that triggers the need for construction work. That is to say, the client's organisation has to respond to certain environmental forces to survive, or to take an opportunity to expand, as a result requiring construction work to be undertaken and therefore providing the process with work to do. It may be that new legislation is enacted, which means that a client's present buildings will not conform, e.g. the requirement for fire safety in hotel buildings; perhaps the client has developed a new production process to compete with his competitors and a new building is needed to house it; a public authority may be required by law to provide a certain new service which requires new buildings. On an international level, internal or external political pressures may mean that a regime has to provide better housing or infrastructure development. In all these examples the need to construct resulted from events outside the client's organisation (or system).

The environment is fundamental not only to triggering the start of the process but also to what takes place within the process of construction. At a strategic level it will determine how the building should be provided. For instance, the state of the property market may have an important effect upon whether a building is leased or a new building is constructed. Such a decision will, of course, also depend upon the process to be housed and whether it requires a new building or can be housed in an existing property. The technology of the process is likely to determine this and will to a large part be dependent upon technological advances in the environment of the client's organisation, for example recently developed materials and machines. Similarly, changes to the proposed building required by the client during design or construction will normally come about in response to environmental forces acting upon the client's organisation.

The environmental forces acting directly on the design and construction process can affect the ability of the process to achieve what the client wants. For example, high economic activity can produce a high level of demand on the construction industry, resulting in shortages of materials, which may delay the project; industrial action can produce labour shortages; a high level and uncertainty of inflation can make estimating and cost control difficult, resulting in overspending.

International projects invariably have extremely complex environments. Not only do the environments generated by the countries in which the projects are being constructed affect them, but also the environments of the countries providing the construction team can have a much more pronounced effect than for locally produced projects for local clients. These influences are reflected in the instability of many developing countries, resulting in the kinds of effect on building projects that occurred in Iran in 1979-80. The action of these forces is also often reflected in material shortages in countries that do not have indigenous material availability and lack control over such supplies.

ENVIRONMENTAL FORCES

An example of how environmental forces may be classified into general groupings is shown in fig. 3.2. These forces are applicable to any system of organisation, and may be interdependent, as illustrated. It is the interdependency of environmental forces that creates complex environments and makes analysis difficult.

A system receives information, energy and material from its environment, transforms them and returns them as output to the environment. Information is received, for example, regarding the economic climate and the opportunities it presents, new technological advances, the skills of people available to the system and the attitudes of trade unions and employers' associations. Energy is received, for instance, through power to drive machines and provide

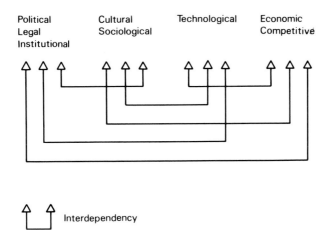

Fig. 3.2   The interdependency of environmental forces.

heat, and through computing power, but perhaps more importantly for the construction system through ideas and people imported into organisations. Material is the raw or partly or fully formed materials used by the system, not only building materials but also those consumed by management and administrative processes.

The output of the construction process is returned to the environment. The effect of this can be visualised, for example, as the use to which the client puts the building and the effect on the community of the establishment of the building in a particular location, and, for commercial clients, the effect of enhanced activities on competitors and the economic climate.

The forces provide their input to the system in a variety of ways, as shown, for example, in fig. 3.3. Environmental forces can be classified in a variety of ways and can be identified and analysed for individual projects. From such an analysis the impact of the forces and their input to the system can be anticipated. This approach will give the manager of the project the best chance of coping with them, although it must be recognised that for many projects it is not possible to mitigate the effect of all environmental forces.

The relative importance of the various environmental forces and their impact upon the client's organisation and the process of construction will vary between different classes of client and project.

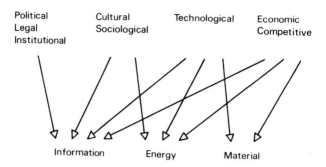

Political   Cultural   Technological   Economic
Legal   Sociological   Competitive
Institutional

Information   Energy   Material

Fig. 3.3   The input of environmental forces.

However, the same classes of environmental force will be acting upon each system and can be broadly visualised through the following examples:

Political

By political forces is meant the influence of government policy, for example control of the level of economic activity through investment and taxation policies, and of the distribution of activity through investment incentives. Political forces influence the availability of finance and exert effects on the labour market. Educational policies are another political force. In countries with unstable regimes, international projects are particularly sensitive to political forces.

Legal

Legislation can affect the client's activities by acting directly on the process of construction (for example, through regulations governing building, safety and planning), or by influencing the incentive to build (for example, by controlling the availability of land). In addition, legislation can affect the relationship of participants (for example, through control of monopolistic activity).

Statutory legislation is the result of political activity, but common law provisions also often have an important effect, particularly overseas. For example, Islamic law based upon the Koran has an important effect upon how disputes in building contracts are settled.

Institutional

Institutional forces include the influence of professional institutions upon the activities of their members through rules of conduct, education, conditions of engagement and fee scales. Trade and employer associations can exert effects on the activities of their members. The influences of the parent company, head office and shareholders are also institutional forces.

An inverse of these effects overseas is the forces acting upon the contributors to projects in which such institutional constraints do not exist, and their need to respond competitively in such circumstances.

Cultural and sociological

The acceptability of specific activities by the general public, particularly as reflected by the local community, is an example of a cultural and sociological force. The effect of events in the world on the values and expectations of employees is another example of this type of force, as is the influence of trade unions and of informal contacts upon members of the system. An example of a significant effect of such forces overseas is that, when building within the walls of the city of Mecca, only Muslims can be employed in any capacity on the site.

Technological

Technological forces include the influence of technology on processes through the development of new materials, techniques and ideas and through the experience of others with those materials, techniques and ideas. The current developments of technology and its potential for solving problems are an obvious example of a technological force. An extremely important influence in this category is the massive increase in cheap computing power now available.

Economic and competitive

Economic and competitive forces include the level of general economic activity and the demands this places upon organisations. The state of competition, the effect of monopolistic phenomena, the availability of finance, materials and labour, and the level of interest rates are other examples of economic and competitive forces. This category is, of course, very closely related to, and dependent upon, political forces.

ACTION OF ENVIRONMENTAL FORCES

The interaction of environmental forces and their consequent effects on the client and the construction process determine the climate in which the system exists. A low level of activity of environmental forces upon a system will lead to a relatively stable system, whereas a high level of activity will lead to the system existing in an uncertain climate.

In terms of the construction process, environmental forces act in two ways:

(a) upon the client's activities and hence transmitted to the construction process (*indirect*);

(b) directly upon the construction process (*direct*).

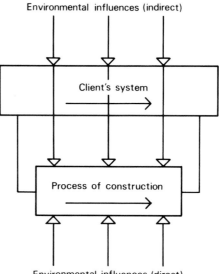

Fig. 3.4   The environment of the process of construction.

The process exists, therefore, in a complex environment, as illustrated in fig. 3.4, which must be reconciled in the interests of the client. In circumstances where the indirect and direct environmental influences act in a conflicting manner, the project management process will be required to attempt to resolve the conflict to the benefit of the client. For example, the contractor may wish to move labour from the site to aid the profitability of another contract (an influence acting directly on the construction process), which may put at risk the completion of the building on time when the client's environment demands completion on time. In such a case it is the duty of the manager of the project to resolve the issue to ensure that this kind of risk will be eliminated.

Environmental influences will be acting directly upon the client's organisation and should determine the organisation structure and mode of operation appropriate to the client's activities. In addition, environmental influences will present opportunities to the client, and will determine the manner in which such opportunities need to be taken. For example, a client's environment may determine that an additional manufacturing capacity needs a building quickly in order to take advantage of an opportunity. In such circumstances, the organisation set up to achieve this must be capable of acting quickly. If, at the same time, forces indicate that uncertainty of the size of the market for the goods is likely, the organisation set up to take advantage of the situation must also be capable of achieving the flexibility required. However, an unexpected large order for the client's goods may make the need for a new building urgent, but it may occur at the time of a rise in activity in the building industry. This may create uncompetitive conditions in terms of price and completion time for projects and makes it difficult to achieve completion when required. Project management must strive to overcome this type of problem caused by conflicting environments.

The construction process is therefore made complex by the type of environment in which it exists, which creates a need for high-level managerial skills. The process must produce a clearly defined solution at the technical level of design and construction but must also remain flexible and adaptive to satisfy environmental requirements. The managing system will be required to reconcile these competing demands, which become more difficult as environmental complexity increases and in many cases may be incompatible.

The ideas developed here see the process of construction as a sub-system of the client's system. As such, it is influenced by the client's environment as well as by the particular environment of the process. This is a development of the tentative view of the Tavistock

Institute,[8] which, although not conceiving the process of construction as a sub-system of the client's system, drew attention to the obsolescent nature of the concept of the architect 'taking a brief from his client' in the conventional way.

Recognition of the construction process as a sub-system of the client's system identifies a boundary between the process and the client's organisation that needs to be integrated. The need for integration has as great an implication for the client as it has for the construction team, since it will demand that both systems establish appropriate ways of achieving the level and style of integration demanded. Both a N.E.D.O. report[9] and the Tavistock study have referred to the lack of such integration in the conventional process and the development of project management skills needs to concentrate upon this aspect.

The implication of the relationship between the systems is that changes in the elements of a client's environment or their relative properties may require a change in how the project is designed, constructed or provided. This may happen during design or even during construction. The integrative device at the boundary between the client's system and the construction system should recognise and take action on changes in the client or construction process environments in terms of maximising the benefit or minimising the deficit to the client. This should be the objective of the integrative device.

The relative uncertainty of environments and the nature of the tasks of both the client's system and the construction system should determine the nature of the integrating device and the organisation structure of the construction process. For example, in an environment that is economically or technologically uncertain or both, the organisation structure of the process should be designed to be sufficiently organic to respond to stimuli. This should be reflected in the style of integration used, for example by the project manager assuming a predominant role. This necessity can be visualised, for example, in large-scale long-programme hospital development. Conversely, a stable environment could more readily accept a more mechanistic organisational structure, with integration based on standard procedures and routines, for example in small school building.

There is no easy or precise method of quantitatively assessing environmental forces and their impact on construction projects. Indeed, if there were, it would be a large step towards solving the problems faced by governments let alone by construction teams! Nevertheless, recognition of environmental forces and an understanding of how they affect construction projects does allow those involved in their management to construct a scenario for their work which should allow them to anticipate and respond to changes in environmental conditions. Preconceived methods of working all too often have fixed rigid patterns for project achievement. This can mean that the process is unable or unwilling to respond to changes to such an extent that although a client's objective may have changed the objective of the construction process has not.

A construction project organisation should therefore be designed to reflect the type of environment in which it is to work. There is little point in using a well tried rigid organisation structure suitable for building public housing for the design and construction of a second Sydney Opera House. The conventional U.K. approach to organisation of the construction process is not directly transportable to overseas projects for similar reasons. The environmental conditions in which such projects are designed and built are very different from those in which the convention was developed.

NEGATIVE ENTROPY, ADAPTATION AND PROTECTED ENVIRONMENTS
Entropy is applicable to all closed physical systems. It is the tendency for any closed system towards a chaotic or disorganised state in which there is no potential for further work.[10] This may sound rather dramatic for a book about construction project organisation but it has some significance. Construction project organisations are open systems and open systems attempt to find ways of avoiding such a fate. They develop negative entropy (negentropy), which is a process of more complete organisation and more ability to transform resources. They achieve this by importing the resources (material, energy, information) from the system's environment. Social organisations such as those involved in construction can continue to import new human and other resources to allow them to continue functioning and may be capable of indefinitely offsetting the entropic process in a way which open biological systems and closed physical systems cannot.

In developing negentropy, an open system may be seeking to achieve a steady state in which the system remains in dynamic equilibrium through the import of resources from its environment. That is, it attains stability or is self-regulating. This view is more relevant to biological systems and allows them to cope with variations in their enviornment. For example, the human body can maintain a steady state in spite of wide variations in the environment. There are of course limits: environmental changes may be so great that the system dies.

Taking these ideas a stage further introduces the adaptive system. A system is adaptive when it changes its own state and/or its environment when there is a change in its environment and/or in its internal state that reduces its efficiency. Adaptation is therefore the ability of a system to modify itself or its environment when either has changed to the system's disadvantage. Complex adaptive open systems allow interchanges among their internal components (or sub-systems) in response to environmental forces to such an extent that the components themselves may change and hence the system as a whole may adapt and so survive.

It is interesting to assess whether the construction process fits into this systems scenario and whether it helps our understanding. The firms that contribute to the construction process do import material from their environments in the form of new staff, new ideas, new technology, etc. and so develop negative entropy. However, construction project organisations are generally temporary. They cease on completion of the project and further organisations will be formed with either the same amalgam of contributors or with different partners. The process itself is not therefore truly negentropic except in the case of 'design-and-build' or turnkey organisations. The firms themselves will, however, be importing from their environments so that they are in a position to be able to join future project organisations. In the case of 'design-and-build' and turnkey organisations, one firm is responsible for practically the whole process and in these cases the firm and the process attempt to develop negentropy.

In adapting to their environment, some systems will attempt to cope with external forces by acquiring control over them. This process can be seen in the mergers of companies, often to reduce competitiveness in their environments, which result in the expansion of the original system. Some organisations may have achieved such a degree of monopoly or have acquired a protected niche in the environment[3] to the extent that they can ignore a certain level of environmental pressure. If this occurs, such organisations can afford to accept a level of suboptimal performance and can survive at that level.

In the case of the construction industry's professional and industrial firms, the amount of adaptation to their environment has not been great, as illustrated by the large proportion of projects still being undertaken on the conventional pattern in spite of much criticism of this process. The conventional pattern of organisation has tended to be self-regulatory and to function to maintain the given structure of the system. This is due, to a large extent, to the system existing in an environment from which it has protected itself. This has been achieved through codes of conduct and fee scales of its professional institutions, which have eliminated, to a large extent, competition between firms, thus enabling the system to resist change and maintain the status quo.

Recent environmental events, for example, the Monopolies Commission review of fee scales and codes of conduct and the increasingly competitive environment in which the system and its clients have to exist, have been significant in beginning to break down such protection. In the case of clients they have brought to bear greater pressure for change in the industry's procedures as a result of the increased competition with which they themselves have been faced. The increasingly multinational nature of the industry's clients and overseas practice have also been major forces for change as clients have experienced methods of managing the construction process that differ from those used conventionally in the U.K.

Although many of the professions' and industry's firms try to protect themselves at an institutional level, changes are taking place at the project level with the use of such processes as management contracting and U.S.A.-style construction management. At the project level it appears that some firms are adapting by changing the nature of the internal components of the building process, for example by introducing the contractor into the design team, and so moving nearer to the open adaptive system described earlier.

In view of the institutional domination of the professions' and industry's firms, it was always likely that adaptation would take place at the project level in response to the demands of clients. However, this is only likely to take place for projects for clients who themselves are adaptive and not protected in some way from their own environments. It is not surprising, therefore, that many initiatives that have taken place in the management of construction projects have been for private commercial or industrial clients, and that there is a lack of stimulus from public clients who are themselves protected to a large degree from their environments. The process of providing a construction project should be an open adaptive system but it may be constrained by the environment within which it exists. Nevertheless, the process needs to change its structure if environmental events, acting either directly upon the process or indirectly upon the client's organisation, dictate that this should happen.

GROWTH, DIFFERENTIATION, INTERDEPENDENCY AND INTEGRATION
Whereas closed systems move towards disorganisation,[12] open systems move in the opposite direction towards a higher level of organisation, which generates greater differentiation among their parts (sub-systems). This feature is observable in business organisation systems and can occur in two ways. One, which has been referred to previously, is when a system seeks to encompass parts of its environment and annexes them as sub-systems, for instance when one firm acquires control of another. The second way by which it occurs is where complex and uncertain environments create the need for sub-systems to specialise further in order to cope with such complexity and uncertainty. That is, the level of skill required is such that a sub-system cannot cope with the range of skills demanded of it and it has to subdivide further. In traditional management thinking, specialisation was considered to be 'a good thing' for increasing the efficiency of undertaking a particular task. Differentiation, however, is now explicitly considered to be necessary in order to allow each sub-system to cope effectively with the part of the system's environment which is acting upon it. Hence, open business organisation systems tend to grow by expansion and by internal elaboration. This is not to say that this is necessarily a benefit in all cases but simply that it is a feature of open systems. It brings along with it the greater management problems of handling large complex systems and hence the need for careful organisation design if such systems are to be effective.

The protected environment of the construction process has limited the impact of these concepts upon it. There have been relatively few examples of growth through amalgamations of firms although there are examples of client organisations acquiring an in-house capacity for designing and constructing projects by taking designers and construction workers on to their payroll. Similarly, a number of consortium firms including architects, quantity surveyors and engineers have been formed. A further example is the growth of design-and-build firms. All of these arrangements help the organisations to handle more easily the environment in which they operate. A growing area of such activity is the joint-venture movement in which firms form separate joint companies to bid for and undertake projects. Companies make such *ad hoc* arrangements between different types of firm, e.g. architects and contractors, and between similar types of firm, e.g. contractors. In most cases the aim is to spread the risk in the difficult and uncertain environmental conditions that usually accompany large and complex projects, which are often overseas.

Growth through internal elaboration has occurred relatively slowly in the construction industry. After many relatively stable years, specialisation into architect, quantity surveyor, specialist engineers and contractors took place quite quickly during the last century and the early 1900s. This resulted from the increasing complexity of the environment in which construction took place during industrialisation. The process then slowed down as the professions protected themselves from their environment and attempted to maintain the status quo. The subsequent proliferation of specialist subcontractors can be seen to be further differentiation to cope with complexity and uncertainty. There is also more recent evidence of the same phenomenon in the specialisation of quantity surveyors into bill of quantities production, construction economics and cost control. Similarly, architects are tending to specialise in particular building types.

The notion of interdependency is explicit in the earlier definition of a system, that is, it is an entity consisting of interdependent parts. If this is the case, then the greater the differentiation of the interdependent parts of a system, the greater will be the need for integration. Differentiation in organisations has been defined[13] as the differences in cognitive and emotional orientations among managers in different functional departments and the differences in formal structure among these departments. Integration has been defined as the quality of the state of collaboration that exists among departments that are required to achieve unity of effort by the environment.

The interdependency of the contributors to the construction process has long been recognised but often as sequential interdependency. In other words, one part cannot act until after the previous part has done its work. It has become increasingly recognised that in fact interdependency should be reciprocal, that is iterative, and the process should move forwards following decisions to which all appropriate parts of the system have made a contribution. The integration of reciprocal interdependencies requires considerably more skill and effort than the integration of sequential interdependencies. It is the recognition of this fact that has focussed attention upon the management needs of projects. Recognition of the need for project management has been highlighted by the complexity and uncertainty of the environment within which construction takes place, which has led to greater differentiation within the construction process and hence to a greater need for skill and effort in integration.

At the extreme of the large complex overseas project it is not unusual to find a number of 'separate' projects going on at the same time using a range of architecture, quantity surveying, engineering and other consultancy firms and a variety of contractors and sub-contractors all working on the same site for the same client who has an overall objective for the development. It is not difficult to visualise the integrating effort required in these circumstances. Nor is this limited to overseas work: some new town developments in the U.K. are not dissimilar. Even at the 'smaller' end of the market, the rehabilitation of an area of a city involves numerous firms all working for a common client with one set of objectives.

FEEDBACK

The concept of feedback is fundamental to understanding how a system is maintained and therefore how it continues to exist and accomplish its purpose. Feedback is the basis of a system's control function. It is through feedback and subsequent action that achieved outcome can be compared with desired outcome so that adjustments in the behaviour of the system can be made. The need for a control function for construction projects is self-evident and much of the energy expended in developing techniques in recent years has been directed at achieving more sophisticated control. However, the type and the amount of feedback designed into a system are the key to the system's stability and economy and in this respect it is interesting to note that the control mechanisms on construction projects are often no more than monitoring devices that declare the position too late after the event to take corrective action, e.g. many 'cost control' procedures. Feedback points should be carefully designed into the system so that appropriate action can be taken at the right time. Feedback should operate on a cost-effective basis in such a way that the value of the control achieved is not cancelled out by the cost of achieving it.

The operation of a feedback loop requires a sample taken at specifically designed points of the system's operation (often referred to as freeze points) to be measured against the objective of the system. For construction projects the sample points need to be chosen on the basis of the nature of the actual project and its environment. That is, for a simple project in a stable environment it is to be expected that only a small number of sample points will be necessary, whereas for a complex project in an uncertain environment, frequent sampling will be required. Naturally, this means that the objective of the system should be appropriately, accurately and explicitly defined to enable the control mechanism to carry out its function. It is questionable whether many of the 'clients' briefs' commonly used in the construction industry are sufficiently clear to allow this to happen. Effective control systems require that the procedure for testing the sample against the objective be designed with appropriate methods of measurement of the sample against the objective and, importantly, with the ability to take action on the basis of feedback information.

The conventional organisational structure of the construction process often does not possess this ability as the relationships of the contributors to the process are arranged in such a way that the people reporting on the current state of the project *vis à vis* its objective are not in a position of sufficient authority to ensure that the project returns to its intended course. This is often a result of the architect being in both an operational capacity as a designer and also in the primary management position for the project. The application of a systems approach to the design of organisations should automatically establish relationships which would allow a properly designed control function with appropriate feedback mechanisms to overcome this deficiency and operate effectively.

The simplest kind of feedback is negative feedback. This enables the control function to correct the system's deviation from course, that is, it encourages a return to the initial objective. Most control functions used on construction projects operate in this way by attempting to correct deviation in cost, time or design of the project and return it to what was intended by the 'client's brief'.

Positive feedback, on the other hand, further amplifies deviation from course. Although this may be an unusual reaction for construction projects, it should not be overlooked. If, during design, it is discovered that the provision of facilities in the project is deviating from what was intended, it may be that the client's original requirements have changed, and upon seeing the developing design the client may decide that he wishes to continue along this course. The objectives would therefore require to be amended in response to positive feedback. Such changes could be as a result of a badly constructed brief but could also be caused by changes in the environment of the client's organisation that have altered his objectives. The control function should therefore operate within the system and between the system and its environment.

The nature of the process of designing and constructing is characterised by a series of 'pinch points' through which it must pass if progress is to be made. At each pinch point a decision has to be made, for example whether the design satisfies the function required of it, whether the cost is acceptable, whether the proposed contractual arrangements will allow the project to be completed on time, etc. The decision points can be conceived as a hierarchy with decisions taken by the client at the top, those taken by the manager of the project at the next level, and those taken by the operational people at the lowest level. The decision structure of a project can be used to provide the control framework. Feedback can take place at each decision point to test whether the proposed decision will help to achieve the objective of the total system. It should be noted that, on many projects, decisions are not made explicit and therefore are not used in this manner. They are not consciously tested but are assumed to be correct as 'that is the way we have always done it'. However, by anticipating decision points and the nature of the decisions to be taken, a control framework could be established and the contribution to be made by each participant could be designed using systems principles.

SUMMARY

The process of designing and constructing a project on behalf of a client can be analysed as an open adaptive system. As such it needs to respond to its environment but in practice it has, to a degree, protected itself from its environment by the construction of rules, procedures and conventions which have been granted validity by public authorities, professional institutions and other bodies associated with construction. Nevertheless, the environmental influences upon the process, particularly those being transmitted to it through its clients, are resulting in the process becoming more responsive.

Analysis in systems terms focusses attention upon the need to bind together the differentiated yet interdependent contributors to the process. This requires a high level of integrative activity which has not traditionally been recognised and provided. The provision of integration must be directed towards the achievement of the total systems objective, which must be stated unambiguously in terms of the client's requirements.

The determining factors of how the system is structured and operates to achieve its objectives are the technical demands of the project, together with the environment in which it is undertaken. The control function should therefore be designed to reflect these factors and be based upon the anticipated decision points in the process. The decision points will determine the interdependency of the contributors to each decision. Therefore their relationships should be designed on systems principles in terms of their contribution to each decision.

Such an analysis demands that the organisational structure established for each project should be developed individually from first principles, and although a range of 'standard solutions' may emerge, it should not be presupposed that any one solution is automatically the correct answer.

Returning, briefly, to the environment and its implication for the construction industry and its professions, it has been observed[10] that industrial companies often fail to obtain adequate information about changes in environmental forces and that it is remarkable how weak they are in their market research departments when they are so dependent upon their market. It has been predicted that organisations will improve their facilities for assessing environmental forces and hence improve their marketing ability. The same could be said of the construction industry and its professions now, and perhaps the same prediction can be made.

The remainder of this book is developed against the background of this systems scenario of the construction process, which can give structure to our understanding of the process. The systems view clarifies how the process works in practice at the present time and points the way to how it may improve in the future to enable it to satisfy more effectively the requirements of its clients.

REFERENCES

1. Ackoff, R.L. (1969) 'Systems, Organisation and Interdisciplinary Research' in *Systems Thinking* ed. Emery, F.E. London: Penguin.
2. Ackoff, R.L. (Nov. 1971) 'Towards a System of Systems Concepts' *Management Science.*
3. Child, J. (1977) *Organisation.* London: Harper and Row.
4. Koontz, H. (Dec. 1961) 'The Management Theory Jungle' *Academy of Management Journal.*
5. Lawrence, P.C. and Lorsch, J.W. (1967) *Organisation and Environment: Managing Differentiation and Integration.* Harvard: Harvard Business.
6. Burns, T. and Stalker, G.M. (1966) *The Management of Innovation.* London: Tavistock Publications.
7. McGregor, D. (1960) *The Human Side of Enterprise.* New York: McGraw-Hill.
8. Crichton, C. *et al.* (1967) *Interdependency and Uncertainty.* London: Tavistock Publications.
9. National Economic Development Office (1975) *The Public Client and the Construction Industries.* London: H.M.S.O.
10. Katz, D. and Kahn, R.L. (1978) *The Social Psychology of Organisations.* 3rd edn. New York: Wiley.
11. Buckley, W. (1968) 'Society as a Complex Adaptive System' in *Modern Systems Research for the Behavioural Scientist: A Sourcebook.* Chicago: Aldine.
12. Kast, F.E. and Rosenzweig, J.E. (1979) *Organisation and Management: A Systems Approach.* 3rd edn. New York: McGraw-Hill.
13. Dalton, G.W., Lawrence, P.C. and Lorsch, J.W. (1970) *Organisational Structure and Design.* New York: Irwin.

4　The Client

INTRODUCTION

On the face of it the term 'the client' is simple enough in the construction industry but its apparent simplicity can hide a quite complex concept. Where the client is to be both owner and occupier of a building, the idea is straightforward but more frequently this is not the case. The owner in the first instance may be a property developer who sells the property to an investment company which then leases it to the occupier. In the public sector the client may be a local authority which receives the finance for the project from central government to implement government policy, and the users may then be a third party, for instance teachers and pupils in the case of a school. There are many more similarly complex cases and thus the first question that needs to be answered is: who is the client?

A construction project team will tend to recognise its client as the body that has the authority to approve expenditure on the project, the form that the project has to take, and its timing (and who pays the fees). The project team will find it simpler if all these authorities are vested in one body but frequently this is not so in practice. For example, central government may allocate funds for a project to a local authority, which will be responsible for developing the project, but it may reserve the right of final approval of both expenditure and aspects of design. A similar situation can occur between head office and regional office of a private client. If another group receives or occupies the building after completion, it will be the client of the client of the construction process, and the responsibility for satisfying that client will rest with the commissioner of the project. Nevertheless, in some instances, the project's client may wish to involve such a third party in approval of the design and this can further complicate identification of the client for the project team.

The members of the project team need to have the ability to understand the structure of their client's organisation, their relationship to others with an interest in the project and what makes them tick. In particular they should understand the decision-making mechanism of the client's organisation and where authority for decisions lies. Only when this is known will the project team be in a position to obtain information upon which it can act with confidence.

Having understood the organisation structure of their client and how it operates, the project team will be in a position to build up the trust and confidence necessary for it to obtain accurate and useful information that will enable it effectively to develop an appropriate brief for the proposed project. Bearing in mind that every company and public authority and even every individual is potentially a client of the construction industry, the breadth of knowledge of organisations required by members of project teams is so vast as to be unrealistic. Project teams therefore need to acquire some conceptual tools with which to analyse and understand their clients' organisations. An indication of the scope of the construction industry and the broad division between its private and public clients is given in table 4.1.

Table 4.1 Distribution of contractors' new orders, Great Britain, 1982 (from reference 1)

	Current prices (£m)	% of all new orders
Public sector		
New housing	984	8.5
Gas, electricity and coalmining industries	380	3.3
Railways and air transport	82	0.7
Education		
Schools	219	1.8
Universities	32	0.3
Health	467	4.0
Offices, factories, garages, shops	584	5.0
Roads	770	6.7
Harbours	95	0.8
Water supply	110	1.0
Sewage disposal	221	1.9
Miscellaneous	574	5.0

Table 4.1 continued

		Current prices (£m)	% of all new orders
Private sector			
New housing		2 928	25.4
Industrial		1 327	11.5
Offices		1 414	12.2
Shops		521	4.5
Entertainment		382	3.3
Garages		134	1.2
Schools and colleges		48	0.4
Miscellaneous		273	2.4
	Total	11 545	

THE INDIVIDUAL CLIENT

The individual client is the exception for most construction projects, particularly where the client is to be both owner and occupier. But even at this level the client can be more complex than expected. A particularly simple example is a couple proposing to have a house built for themselves. In such a situation there is a direct relationship between the clients and the leader of the project team, and communication of information should be straightforward. However, even at this level it can become complicated. Who is the client: the husband, who may be providing the finance, or his wife who will probably be the main user, particularly in the kitchen (or vice versa, to avoid being sexist)? Relationships between married couples vary considerably so the project team needs to understand the particular relationship, which could be difficult! This may be taking the point a bit too far, but it illustrates the problem.

A similar but amplified situation occurs in the case of the sole owner of a business. In this case the relationship between the owner and his employees is important. Will the owner instruct the project team alone or will his workforce also be involved? Is the owner able to indicate clearly to the project team the activities to be housed or will the workforce need to be consulted? If they need to be consulted, what does the team do if the owner is not sympathetic to their views? Even at this relatively simple level the way in which the team obtains the information it needs can depend upon understanding the client's activities, organisation and relationships.

THE CORPORATE CLIENT

The broad classification of corporate client includes all companies and firms controlled other than by a sole principal. This group therefore covers all companies from the small, simply structured organisation to the massive multinational corporation. The myriad of functions, sizes and structures of firms within this group poses particular problems for the project team. If it is to carry out its work well, the team will need to understand the objectives of the corporate client, and these will often be complex. In particular, it will need to understand the purpose of the project for which it has been commissioned and how it is intended to contribute to achieving the client's long-term objectives. To understand the objectives of the client, and to establish the firm's objectives, it will have to be familiar with how the client's organisation operates. Such knowledge is also required to identify where the best information is likely to be available on which to base the project proposal. It will also be necessary for the project team to be able to assess the ability and status of the members of the client's organisation who are transmitting the information to them.

As no two clients within this group are likely to be structured identically, the organisation analysis skill demanded of the project team is very high indeed. Coupled with this is the need for the team to be able to build up and maintain the confidence of the client, for only if this exists is the team likely to be able to obtain the information it needs to do its job effectively, much of which may be of a confidential nature.

Perhaps the only common component of such companies is that final authority will lie with the board of directors or equivalent group and in some companies it may in reality lie with only one member of the board or with a small group of directors. The leader of the project team will have to cultivate confidence at this level. Nevertheless, in the more complex company interrelationships that frequently exist, it may be that full authority does not lie with the board but with a board of another company which has control of the client's company. Such situations can make it very difficult for the project team to proceed with confidence as decisions may be overturned to the serious detriment of progress on the project.

Frequently the project team will have to talk to a large number of people in the client's company to tease out the brief for the project and to develop it into an acceptable final proposal. This does not have to be restricted to managers but may also include the operational people in the company. Often the client may not know clearly what he requires. The briefing process requires a large number of important decisions to be made by the client and the source and authority of such decisions have to be identified. These decisions are not just about the functional attributes of the building but most importantly about the time scale and budget for the project. Of particular importance is the timing of decisions by the client on important aspects of the project, e.g. budget approvals, as the incidence of decisions will have a fundamental effect on the progress of the project.

It is not uncommon to find that the client's company will appoint a project co-ordinator from the company to act as the link between the client and the project team. This has been found to work successfully but it does, of course, depend predominantly upon the quality of the person appointed. What is of vital importance is the authority of the person in this position. If members of the project team are to rely on his instructions, they need to be sure that he has the authority of the board to issue instructions to them. If he has not, then the result will probably be frustration, delay and abortive work. The ground rules need to be clearly laid down with the client's board of directors at a very early stage. This presents a very real problem as the project team is likely to be rather diffident about 'pushing too hard' for fear of offending an important client and this is often linked with a reluctance to pry into the client's affairs, although both are necessary if an acceptable project is to be realised effectively.

Dealing with a client can be a very frustrating business, particularly in the case of large clients, which tend to move towards a bureaucratic form of organisation. This can result in the project team adopting procedures that result in their designing what they think the client wants without basing it upon investigation of what the client needs. The orientation of the project team should be strongly towards finding out rather than constructing a series of cockshies for the client to criticise. This demands skills of investigation and a large measure of diplomacy.

THE PUBLIC CLIENT

Public clients include all the publicly owned organisations that have the authority to raise finance to commission construction work. In all such cases the funds will normally be raised by taxation or in the money market on the authority of the government. They include local authorities, nationalised industries, government agencies and the government itself. Normally, authority to spend money on construction stems from the government but usually, when authority has been given, the 'client' may control the spending of money within certain constraints, although withdrawal of authority is not unknown.

Many of the features described above for the corporate client are applicable to public clients, particularly nationalised industries, but the situations encountered are often more closely constrained and difficult through having to work through committees whose authority may not be clearly defined. The bureaucratic rules that surround most decisions to construct for public clients can often lead to an inefficient construction process. A common example is the establishment and approval of a budget for a project and the limitation of having to place the construction contract during a particular financial year. This approach can produce situations in which the cash flow and budget are inflexible, and so may inhibit the project team's ability to obtain value for money, particularly where virement between different expenditure headings is prohibited. Similarly, value for money may be difficult to achieve if a project has to be rushed in order to meet a financial-year deadline.

Such difficulties may have to be faced within a structure which requires that the project team is instructed by officers of the public body who are subject to control by a committee of elected or appointed representatives. They themselves may be controlled by higher level committees, either within the public body and/or within government. The process may also include the involvement of central government officials. In such circumstances the difficulty of knowing just where the decision making is done can be a severe problem.

The project team has to develop skills in understanding how such organisations work. The wide range of public clients and their objectives, many of which may be politically generated, place great demands of client analysis on the project team. Objectives can be difficult to pin down and unresolved conflicts may exist between the various client interests and the potential users of the project. If final authority in such situations rests with an elected committee, the outcome may be unpredictable and the project team will be faced with uncertainty.

As with corporate clients, there can be great benefit in working through a co-ordinator from the client's organisation provided that his authority is clearly stated and understood by both the client and the project team. The ground rules for the validity of information and decisions have to be laid down at an early stage, but even the ground rules may not be protected if there is a change in policy, often resulting from a change in composition of the elected committee who have final authority over the project.

Uncertainty and complexity stemming from the nature of the client body is compounded on overseas projects because of the project team's unfamiliarity with the client's organisation. Many of the differences arise for historical or cultural reasons. A significant amount of homework needs to be undertaken on both the influences at work in the country as a whole and on the culture and attitudes of each client.

CLIENTS' OBJECTIVES

The most important feature of any building project should be the client's objectives in embarking on the construction of the project. The need for the project will normally have arisen from some demand arising from the client organisation's primary activity. For example, the client's primary activity may be food processing. In order to remain competitive the client may need to absorb within the firm work previously subcontracted, which may require construction work to be undertaken. A client with a plant located overseas may wish to provide it with its own power supply in the event of an unstable political situation threatening existing sources. The client may be an education authority and there may be a demand for additional school places, which have to be provided by the construction of a new school. A health authority may be required to respond to advances in medical science by providing a new treatment facility.

A client's need will therefore be stimulated by the environment of his organisation, which will present opportunities to which he responds. Such external stimuli may be economic forces, which give the opportunity for profit, or sociological forces, which present the chance to respond to a social need, but more usually they are combinations of different classes of stimulus. The basic response of a client to environmental forces is the result of his need to survive; above this level the client responds in order to expand as a result of his drive and motivation. Survival is the basic objective of the client and can be defined as maintaining his position relative to those of his competitors. This is more easily conceived for commercial organisations but it is also true for public clients. In commercial terms it requires sufficient response to stay in business. In terms of non-profit organisations, it means sufficient response to prevent the organisation being replaced by some other mechanism: for example, the recent establishment of urban development corporations to undertake some of the work of certain local authorities. A further example is the establishment of housing associations to provide some public housing previously provided by local authorities.

The effect of forces in the client's environment will therefore trigger the start of the construction process although it may not be realised at the time that a project is needed and at that stage it is unlikely that any member of the project team will be involved. When it becomes apparent that a construction project is needed to satisfy the client's objectives, the brief begins to be formed. A common major problem is that the project team will normally not be involved at this early stage and a number of important decisions which may inappropriately constrain the design of the project may have been made by the time they are brought in.

The client's brief is often perceived as a reasonably detailed statement of what the client requires but it is important that the strategic level of the brief is not overlooked at the expense of detail. The client will be concerned in the three major areas of price, quality and time. The weight different clients give to each of these factors will vary. They will require value for money but on their own particular terms. A public client with a low capital budget but high revenue budget may wish to suppress the initial price at the expense of quality; a client building a prestigious building may prefer the opposite; a client in a rich, developing country may see the time for completion as paramount at the expense of price but not of quality, and so on.

Quality and price can be subdivided into components, each of which will have its own weighting within the balance which a particular client wishes to achieve between competing factors.

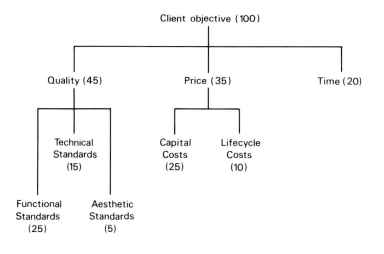

Fig. 4.1 Client objectives - weighting of factors.

A summary of a typical weighting is illustrated in fig. 4.1. The balance which the client requires may not be possible and compromise between conflicting factors may have to be negotiated. For instance, it would be illogical to have a low weighting for technical standards and a high weighting for low life cycle costs.

This type of strategic scenario will be required as a backcloth against which the detailed brief can be prepared. The client's priorities will therefore have to be established. It may well be that there is conflict within the client's organisation regarding priorities. The project team will need to be confident that it has interpreted the balance properly and to achieve this it will have to understand the client's organisation, its decision-making process and where its highest authority lies. It will be against such a concept that the client will ultimately judge his satisfaction with the completed project and upon which the reputation of the project team will rest. This is not to say that it is easy to make clients understand the conflicting pressures of a construction project. Most clients would expect each component to be weighted at 100%. Given unlimited capital this may be possible, but is not the reality of most construction projects.

RELATIONSHIP OF THE CLIENT'S ORGANISATION AND THE CONSTRUCTION PROCESS

An organisation can be considered as an open adaptive system in terms of a general input-output model as in fig. 4.2. Both the client's organisation and the construction project organisation can be considered in this manner.

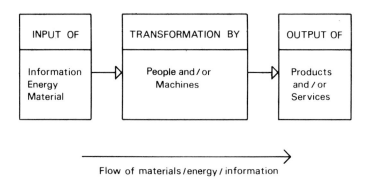

Fig. 4.2   General model of an organisation as an open system.

An open system is in continual interaction with its environment and retains the capacity for work or energy transformation. A system must receive sufficient input of resources from its environment to maintain its operations and also to export the transformed resources to the environment in sufficient quantity to continue the cycle. For example, the client's organisation, whether private or public, receives inputs from society (its environment) in the form of people, materials, money, information, etc. It transforms these into outputs of products, services and rewards to the organisational members that are sufficiently large to maintain their participation. The output is therefore returned to society (the environment) in some form. The project organisation performs in the same way although the nature of the inputs and outputs differs.

In chapter 1 it was suggested that the management system of an organisation could be seen to consist of:

(a)   the organisation sub-system;
(b)   the behavioural sub-system;
(c)   the technical sub-system;
(d)   the decision-making sub-system.

The technical sub-system is defined by the technology required to undertake the task of the organisation and is represented by the skills, knowledge and equipment required and the way in which they have to be used. Although it can be developed and adapted by the organisation, it is frequently prescribed by the current external state of development of the particular process. The technical sub-system is that to which the behavioural sub-system has to relate and with which it must be integrated. The behavioural sub-system will have a significant influence on the effectiveness of the utilisation of technology. The organisation sub-system is the structure that relates the technical to the behavioural sub-systems, and the decision-making sub-system is the mechanism through which the managing system activates the organisation.

The implication of this scenario is that analysis of the technical system will produce a systematic picture of the tasks and task relationships of an organisation to which the other sub-systems relate. Such a view of a client's organisation allows the project team to understand the *modus operandi* of its client's organisation and gives it a basis for integration during the construction process. The technical sub-system of a client can be readily perceived in manufacturing industry (e.g. manufacturing vehicles, electrical components, producing oil, etc.) but it is equally applicable to non-manufacturing activities, for example treating patients (health authority), collecting taxes (inland revenue), designing advertisements (advertising agency), etc.

This scenario also applies to the construction process itself. The technical sub-system is the technology required for designing and constructing the project. The behavioural sub-system is the attitudes and values of the members of the process. The organisation sub-system is the way in which they relate to each other and the decision-making sub-system is the mechanism through which the process moves forward. The technical sub-system dominates and in this respect it is important to recognise the differences in the technical sub-systems between construction projects. For example, the technical sub-system for the construction of a house is quite different from that for a multistorey car park, a theatre or a power station, and so on. It therefore follows that the organisation and decision-making sub-systems should be designed to reflect the technical and behavioural sub-systems. This demands that a variety of organisation solutions should be available to suit the particular project. There are therefore two systems involved, that of the client and that of the construction process, and they become joined temporarily for the duration of the project. The construction process becomes a temporary sub-system of the client's organisation, as shown in fig. 4.3.

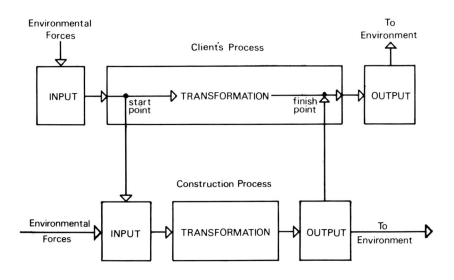

Fig. 4.3   An input-output model of the process of providing a project.

The client's primary activity can be seen as an input-transformation-output system and a response to environmental forces triggers the start point of the construction process. A part of the input to the client's primary activity (e.g. money, energy) is diverted to become an input to the construction process, which will also acquire other inputs directly from its environment. In both cases the inputs can be summarised as materials, information and energy. (Energy is the input that drives the transformation process and therefore includes people, ideas, power, etc.) The output of the construction process will then return to the transformation process of the client's system to provide an additional facility, which will contribute to his primary activity and assist in achieving his objectives. The construction process can therefore be conceived as an internal transformation within the client's system and as a temporary sub-system of it.

CONFLICTING OBJECTIVES

It has been widely recognised that business organisation systems tend to have multiple objectives and that some form of compromise takes place. Multiple objectives arise as a result of the network of relationships that exist within a system. This is particularly to be expected for construction projects owing to the client-construction process relationship and the fact that the construction process itself often consists of a number of organisationally independent firms. The benefit of taking a systems view is that the conflicting multiple objective situation can be made explicit.

Multiple objectives arise because of the individual aspirations of the sub-systems (e.g. firms or departments), which tend to develop their own purpose outside the main purpose of the system. It is therefore important to identify and relate a system to predominant objectives. In terms of the client-construction process relationship, the predominant objective must be that of the client, which will reflect the primary function of his organisation.

One of the tasks of the management process is to ensure that sub-systems remain orientated to the primary function of the system. A company must be sure that its sub-systems (e.g. departments) are not developing discrete objectives that conflict with the company's primary objective. A good example of this is what is often referred to as 'empire building', in which the manager of a department is concerned only with building up his own department irrespective of optimising its contribution to the firm. The possibility of conflicting objectives in the construction process is even more likely as not only may the client's sub-systems develop discrete objectives and try to implement them during the briefing of the project team, but the sub-systems (e.g. firms) making up the project team may also develop discrete objectives that conflict with the client's objectives. An important role of project management will be to ensure that the objectives of the client are accurately and clearly stated and that all the contributors to the project remain orientated towards them.

The primary function of the client's organisation will be that process which it continuously undertakes in order to survive as an organisation. The construction process has its own primary function which is providing the project, which should remain compatible with the primary function of the client. Circumstances may arise in which the primary function of the construction process temporarily becomes the primary function of the client's system but normally it will remain subservient to it. For example, if it is known that the only way by which the client's firm can survive is by completing and commissioning a building so that a particular process can come on stream by a particular date, the client's primary function will, temporarily, be to ensure that this happens. A danger following a temporary shift of the primary function is that it may lead to a permanent redefinition to the detriment of an organisation's ability to survive. Similarly, if the leaders or members of an enterprise do not agree on their definition of the primary function, the survival of the enterprise will be at risk.

Orientation of the construction process towards its objective of providing what the client requires is achieved through feedback. The client's objective for his project and the details of how this is to be achieved should be stated in the brief. Feedback loops should be designed into the construction process to establish whether the output of the process is compatible with the brief. Such feedback points should coincide with the major decision points in the process and be designed to ensure that any additional information arising from the environment during design and construction that may require the brief to be amended is taken into account.

PROJECT CHANGE

Most construction projects are designed and constructed in accordance with the brief established early in the process, but the project team needs to be aware that uncertainty and change in the client's environment may require that alterations have to be made to the project in order to respond to them. The R.I.B.A. Plan of Work[2] indicates a time after which the project design should not be changed. This is rather idealistic as it is surely not reasonable or sustainable to try and tell a client who is investing a considerable amount of money that the design cannot be changed when the circumstances in which he is operating have altered significantly.

An understanding of the state of the client's environment is necessary for the project team, since, in conditions of uncertainty of the client's needs, flexibility must be maintained. This may be achieved, for example, by not selecting a long-term fixed solution such as a new building, or by designing a building that exhibits the flexibility demanded by the environment. The implication of this is that the maximum amount of up-to-date information regarding the requirements of the client must be maintained when the project is being designed. For example, an advance in technology for a particular process (e.g. high-rise fork-lift truck design) could mean that significant amendments to the brief should be made to take advantage of such developments.

Conversely, changes in the environment of the construction process should be allowed to amend the structure of the process if this can be done to the advantage of the client. The members of the project team should keep themselves aware of any such changes and be ready to advise their client accordingly. For example, shortage of steel could result in a change of design or in ordering the steel prior to signing of the main building contract, or in bringing forward the commencement of construction by adopting innovative approaches to appointing a contractor.

ROLE OF THE CLIENT

The degree of involvement and the role of the client in the construction process will depend to a large extent upon:

(a) the structure of the client's organisation;
(b) the client's knowledge and experience of the construction process;
(c) the authority vested in the various levels of the client's organisation;
(d) the personal characteristics of the client's people who have responsibility for the project.

If the client constructs frequently, he will probably have employees familiar with the process who can act as co-ordinators on his behalf and who will liaise within his organisation and between it and the project team. In such a case the client will maintain a presence close to the project. The effectiveness of this arrangement will depend on the degree of authority vested in such a co-ordinator. If this is high, it will be to the advantage of the project provided that the co-ordinator has personal skills and characteristics that gain the confidence of the project team. In these circumstances the delegation of authority to the manager of the project team by the client will not need to be high. On the other hand, if the co-ordinator does not possess much authority and/or his personal characteristics are not suitable, this arrangement may be counterproductive as it could lead to frustration and delay.

The authority of the co-ordinator will depend upon the authority pattern within the client's organisation. If the organisation is mechanistic, it is probable that authority will not be delegated to any great degree. The project team will therefore have to rely on the higher levels of the client's organisation for decisions. This could result in delay in reaching decisions, as it is unlikely that people at such a level in the client's organisation would have sufficient time in addition to their other activities to devote to keeping close to the project. If, however, the client's organisation is structured so that authority is delegated well down the organisation, a member of the client's staff who is intimately involved with the particular project may have authority over most matters. This should result in close integration of the client organisation and the construction process, with the effect that decisions can be readily obtained to the advantage of that process.

Much has been written about the amount of authority which the 'project manager' should or should not be given. In the context of a project manager who is external to the client's organisation, this is a difficult decision for the client. The project team will be spending a large amount of the client's money and human nature does not normally allow some external agency the authority to do this. Nevertheless, in such complex circumstances as a construction project, such decisions have to be faced and resolved. Much will depend upon the structure of the client's organisation and his experience of construction. As referred to earlier, if the client appoints his representative from within his organisation and gives him a large degree of authority, then the manager of the project team should not require much authority as he should have easy access to the client's representative. On the other hand, if the client keeps authority for the project high in his organisation, he should consider vesting significant authority in the manager of the project team. The problems start to arise when neither of these situations exists.

Similarly, problems will arise when authority is not clearly defined as often happens when the client fudges both authority and responsibility for the project within his organisation. This usually 'knocks on' to an unclear statement of the authority of the manager of the project team. Problems then manifest themselves as either decisions not taken at the right time or even not at all, or in decisions being frequently changed leading to delay and abortive work.

There is no set solution to the integration of the client and the construction process. Each mechanism will have to be designed to suit the particular organisation of the client body. The client cannot be expected to change his organisation structure fundamentally because he is temporarily embarking on construction. Therefore the mechanism should reflect his organisation, yet clearly state the pattern of authority and responsibility for the project. Only from this basis can the decision-making process and communication system for the project be identified. The integration of the client and the project team is a most significant factor in the success of the project and requires understanding and skill in its design.

REFERENCES

1. Housing and Construction Statistics (March 1983). No. 13, Pt. 2. London: H.M.S.O.
2. *Handbook of Architectural Practice and Management* (1980). London: Royal Institute of British Architects.

5 The Project Team

Reference was made in chapter 1 to the large number of firms involved in the construction process. These firms are usually independent units which are interdependent in terms of the work they undertake - the design and production of construction work. Even so they vary considerably in the range and quality of skills they offer. The number of different combinations of firms that may be involved in a construction project is therefore very large. As a result, firms have to be familiar with working with a variety of other firms, and at any one time within a particular firm many different amalgams of firms will be working on the projects in hand.

Table 5.1 gives some examples of the types of amalgam that may exist, and the additional variety introduced by the various ways by which the construction contract may be awarded. The table illustrates eighteen primary examples of different arrangements, but many more variations are available. Each of the different arrangements generates a different set of relationships between the contributors. At any given time a person can find himself involved in a variety of situations as it is not unusual for someone to be working on a number of projects simultaneously. The complexity of the situation is compounded by the variety of clients and projects which overlie the professional relationships.

Within the amalgams shown in table 5.1, management takes place at various levels. In each case the individual contributing firms have to be managed. The partners or directors will be concerned to maximise the efficiency of their firm while at the same time enhancing its reputation for service. The same will also apply to departments of public authorities. If firms are concerned with more than one skill, e.g. a professional consortium and local authority architects' departments, this will involve managing not only the individual skills but also the collective skills of the members. Within

Table 5.1 Examples of amalgams of firms

Designers \\ Contractor	Appointed by competition after design is substantially completed	Appointed by negotiation or competition early in design process	Management contract	'In house' to client	Design-and-build
General practice surveyor, architect, quantity surveyor, structural engineer, service engineer, all in separate private practices	X	X	X		
As above, plus a project manager in separate practice	X	X	X		
Consortium of design skills including project manager and separate general practice surveyor firm	X	X	X		
All design skills 'in house' to client (e.g. local authority, private developer), including project manager	X	X	X	X	
Some design skills including project manager, 'in house' to client with others in separate private practices	X	X	X	X	
'In house' to contractor					X*

*In addition the client may appoint consultants to oversee the contract on his behalf individual firms, the service provided to a particular project will have to be managed within the context of the total firm. Resources will have to be allocated to satisfy the demands of the project and also be within the capacity of the firm, and decisions regarding both the quality and quantity of resources allocated must be made. For example, the services engineer will have to manage the services engineering provisions within the resources of the services engineering practice, the contractor the construction process, etc. At a lower level each individual contributor will have to manage his own contribution. All these activities will have an objective in terms of satisfying the client, but they will also have other objectives. The dominant one will be to ensure a profit for their firm (this also applies to public authorities in terms of effectiveness) while at the same time maintaining the firm's reputation. Individuals will have personal objectives (e.g. self advancement, avoidance of responsibility). While the objectives of the firm, the project and the individuals continue to be satisfied simultaneously, all will be well. However, if these objectives clash, it is the role of the manager of the project on behalf of the client to resolve the conflict in the client's interest.

Project management is the management of the contributors to the project who will be from different firms except where they are totally 'in-house' to the client's organisation. Its sole objective is the satisfactory completion of the project on behalf of the client. It therefore normally crosses firms' boundaries and for its purposes temporary management structures are created for the duration of the project. They will be disbanded on completion of the project but may be re-formed for future projects. It is important that the contributing firms recognise the existence of temporary management structures and organise themselves so that their members become full members of those structures. This requires that firms be prepared to dedicate staff to projects even though this may at times appear to be to the detriment of the internal organisation of the firm. Firms should therefore be structured to allow staff to give allegiance to the projects on which they are employed and to be involved with only the number of projects that allows them to devote sufficient time to each. Dedication to projects should enhance a firm's reputation, and dedication to firms should enhance profit in the short run. If both are not achievable, a trade-off between them takes place to the detriment of one or both. Such a situation demands sensitive and skilful management if both reputation and profit are to be optimised and if staff are to be motivated and retain job satisfaction. Staff should be seen to be rewarded for achieving the appropriate balance.

RELATIONSHIP WITH THE CLIENT

The complexity of project management structures raises the issue of how best the project team should be integrated with the client's organisation. The two ends of the spectrum are illustrated by, at one end, the project manager or other leader of the project team as the only point of contact between the team and the client, with all instructions and advice being passed through this channel. At the other end, all members of the project team have direct access to the client and in this arrangement the leader of the project team co-ordinates the instructions and advice given. Either of these alternatives is likely to be unsatisfactory in most cases and the appropriate integrating mechanism will probably lie somewhere between.

The design of the mechanism will be dependent to a large degree on the amount of authority delegated by the client to the manager of the project team. Where substantial authority is delegated, most of the contact between the client and the project team is likely to be directly with the manager of the project team acting as the surrogate client. In such cases, for aspects for which the manager of the team does not have authority to act, the client may well prefer the leader of the project team alone to present recommendations to him. In cases where the manager has little authority, the client may prefer to thrash out issues in consultation with all or some of the members of the project team. Alternatively, the client may require the project team manager to make recommendations for his decision, so that the client can discuss them with the whole group. In this arrangement, although the manager may not have delegated authority from the client, he gains significant authority from being in the position of co-ordinating and influencing the proposition(s) that form the basis of recommendations to the client. In putting propositions and recommendations to the client, the project team manager will also be in a good position, even in the presence of other members of the team, to influence the final outcome.

Where there is direct access by team members to the client, the team manager will need to ensure that the client receives a balanced view and that decisions are made in the light of all the factors affecting the project, rather than as a result of the statements of the strongest personality in the team. For example, many construction projects do not have a formal, detailed brief. The detailed brief emerges through the architect placing a series of sketch designs before the client, which are amended or rejected. The 'brief' therefore proceeds incrementally until the client 'sees what he requires' on the drawings. In such a process it is essential that the other members of the team be present and involved. Otherwise important elements, such as cost and time constraints and certain significant elements of design (e.g. aspects of services), may be ignored through concentrating attention upon other aspects. The result could be that a building is proposed which the client cannot afford and which, by that stage of design, cannot be amended in time to be completed to programme. Such a development is potentially more likely if the architect or other professional contributor is also the project team manager than if the leader were independent of the professional contributors.

There can be no hard and fast rules laid down for integration with the client. So much will depend upon the particular views held by the client and his experience of construction projects. However, the project team manager can influence most clients and should ensure that whatever is devised is clearly laid down and understood by everyone involved, particularly the client. The essence of the integration is that the decisions made as a result of contact with the client are controlled in terms of the objectives of the project. Unilateral decisions made by either the client or one of the team can, at best, lead to confusion which will take a great deal of unravelling and cause abortive work. At worst they may be incorporated into the project, with the result that whereas they may satisfy one aspect of the project's objectives, they defeat one or more of the client's other objectives, which in the long run may be more significant to the client's satisfaction with the total project.

DIFFERENTIATION, INTERDEPENDENCY AND INTEGRATION

The specialisation of the contributors to construction projects has been occurring throughout the world since the last century. As observed in chapter 2, in the U.K. from the basis of architect/builder have evolved quantity surveyors, various specialist engineers, general contractors, specialist subcontractors and general practice surveyors.

Even within these specialist occupations there are often further specialist subdivisions. For instance, there are design architects, detailing architects and job architects; in the quantity surveying field there are building economists, bill preparers and final account specialists. Whereas on some projects the same person may undertake all the functions of a particular contributor, for many projects a number of people are involved at the different stages of a particular specialist contribution. Add to this the way in which clients' organisations are often subdivided into specialist groups, all of which have a contribution to make in terms of project specification, and the complexity of the interrelationships that emerge is clearly evident. In systems terminology such specialisation is called differentiation,[1] which can be defined in construction terms as the difference in cognitive and emotional orientation among contributors to projects who offer specialist skills. The differences in cognitive and emotional orientation of the specialists within the construction process are readily apparent. Each of the specialists tends to view his or her colleagues with a certain amount of scorn. The contractor rarely expresses respect for the architect and vice versa, and no one has a good word for the quantity surveyor or consulting engineer! The divisions are wide and need to be recognised as such. Continuing efforts are being made at a national level to resolve differences in perception, but at a project level there exists a pressing need to ensure that such differences are reconciled so that they do not affect the performance of the project team to the detriment of the project and hence the client.

Closely related to the concept of differentiation is the concept of sentience, developed by the Tavistock group.[2] A sentient group is one to which individuals are prepared to commit themselves and on which they depend for emotional support. In the construction process this can arise from allegiance to a firm or to a profession or to both. It is a particularly strong force in the construction process and it is from sentience that the perception of the process by the different contributors arises. It has been found that sentience is likely to be strongest where the boundaries of a sentient group and of a task coincide. This is the usual situation in the construction process. For instance, architects are normally solely involved in architecture and builders in building, with very little, if any, overlap. The various contributors have a tendency to focus upon and be concerned only with their own specialism and are unable to perceive and respond to the problems of others.

Sentience is weakest in a group of unskilled or semi-skilled workers whose roles are interchangeable and where each individual is dispensable. Individuals in such a group will not acquire sentience unless the group finds supplementary activities through which members can make individual and complementary contributions. It has been found that sentience is strongest in members of a professional body that confers upon its members the right to engage in professional relations with clients in which task and sentient boundaries coincide. There is a specific danger when both direct relations with clients and coincidence of boundaries of sentient and task groups occur in that it may produce a group that becomes committed to a particular way of doing things. Although both efficiency and satisfaction may be greater in the short run, in the long run such a group is likely to inhibit change and behave as though its objective had become the defence of an obsolescent method of working. This view appears to have some significance for the construction process. There have been many pleas over the years for the boundaries between the professions of the building industry to be broken down but there is still little evidence of this having taken place on any appreciable scale.

The differentiation of skills together with their reinforcing sentience, can be clearly seen in the construction industry. It is also quite clear that all the contributors, each in his own 'box', are interdependent in carrying out their work of producing the completed project to the client's satisfaction. The network of interdependencies is practically total. It is not that each contributor is dependent on one other but that all contributors are in some way dependent upon all the others. If members of the process were asked if they were interdependent, they would undoubtedly agree, but this is not something that would be at the forefront of their minds if the question were not asked. This lack of recognition of interdependency begins with the education of members of the construction process. Each discipline is educated in relative isolation from the others. Exceptionally there may be some joint work, but if so it is only likely to be a very small proportion of the time devoted to study. The difficulties of resolving this situation are compounded by different patterns of courses and a lack of will to break the mould and reform the educational process. This problem is particularly apparent in the U.K. but is common throughout the world.

The contributors are interdependent because on the one hand the various tasks that have to be undertaken to achieve the finished project require an input from a range of contributors, and on the other hand because the tasks themselves are interdependent as frequently a task cannot be commenced until another has been completed or unless another task is undertaken in parallel. Different types of interdependency exist and have been classified as pooled, sequential and reciprocal.[3]

Pooled interdependency is basic to any organisation. Each part renders a discrete contribution to the whole. The parts do not have to be operationally dependent upon or even interact with other parts, but the failure of any one part can threaten the whole and therefore the other parts, for example the decentralised divisions of a large, diversified company. In the construction process, if one part fails, it will not necessarily mean the failure of the other parts but the failure may reflect upon the reputation of the other parts. *Sequential interdependency* takes a serial form. Direct interdependency between the parts can be identified and the order of the interdependency can be specified. For example, bills of quantities must be prepared before tenders can be invited (using this particular form of procedure). *Reciprocal interdependency* is when the outputs of each part become the inputs for the others and the process moves forwards through a series of steps. Each step requires interaction between the parts and each part is penetrated by the others. This is seen, for example, when preparing an outline proposal for a building which must be functionally and aesthetically sound and also feasible from a structural and cost point of view.

The three types of interdependency can be arranged in ascending order of complexity as pooled, sequential and reciprocal. A more complex type also contains the less complex types. The order of complexity is also the order of most difficulty of integration. If, therefore, there are different types of interdependency, there would need to be different methods of integration. As reciprocal interdependency is the most difficult to integrate, and as this type of interdependency dominates in the construction process, the integrative mechanisms and effort need to be of a high order.

It has been found that the integration of pooled interdependency is best achieved through standardisation and formal rules, and sequential interdependency through planning. That is, the tasks to be undertaken can be anticipated and their sequence planned so that sequential interdependency is identified and recognised at an early stage. The managing process should then ensure that integration takes place as planned. Reciprocal interdependency is integrated by mutual adjustment and feedback between the parts involved.

The integration of reciprocal interdependency requires close association between interdependent parts to ensure that the required input takes place at the appropriate time and that account is taken of the various inputs in the process. The management of reciprocal interdependencies requires that a balance be maintained between the inputs in terms of clients' objectives. A clear perception of clients' objectives is required, together with the diplomacy and expertise necessary to integrate a group of highly skilled professionals.

In an organisation which is strongly differentiated yet largely interdependent, such as that found for construction projects, the key to success is the quality and extent of the integrative effort provided by the managers of the organisation. The root of project management should therefore be the integration of the organisation. This applies whatever the organisation structure adopted. Within any organisation there will be someone, or some group, responsible for managing the process. Conventionally, the architect both de-signed and managed. More recently, a project manager has frequently been appointed to manage the process. In either of these cases, or any other, the manager's fundamental activity is integration.

Integration will be necessary in two specific directions. One is the integration of the people involved with each specific task. At a basic level the manager will need to ensure that the appropriate people with the right skills are involved at the correct time. This may seem obvious but it is surprising how often this does not happen. If advice is given too late in the process, or if it is not given at all or not taken, it can lead to abortive work or delay and dissatisfaction by the client with the outcome of the project. So within each task the integration of the contributors needs to be ensured. This type of integration is achieved at a personal level through the characteristics of the manager. He should create in the project team recognition and respect for the contribution of others by all members so that the member responsible for carrying out a specific task automatically seeks advice. The manager should then monitor progress within tasks to ensure that the development of the project reflects the level of response between contributors that he considers to be necessary.

The other, and equally important, need for integration is between the output of the tasks. Each task undertaken by the project team will have to be compatible with each other and in relation to the project's objectives. The manager of the process, who should be taking an overview of the various tasks being undertaken, should evaluate the output of the tasks in terms of their compatibility. This will require what is in effect a feedback loop at each output at which the latter is 'measured' against the project objectives and against the output of other tasks. For instance, it is unacceptable for the design of the electrical services to satisfy the client's objectives for power and lighting if the proposed solution cannot be provided within the cost limit for the work. Adjustment would have to be made to the design, the cost limit, or the client's objectives. Sound integration within tasks should be designed to prevent such an occurrence, but integration of the output (between tasks) acts as a 'backstop' with formal feedback opportunities to ensure that within-task integration has taken place effectively.

The integrative mechanisms designed into the organisation structure will depend on the particular project and its environment, but will range from integration through personality to formal and rigorous feedback mechanisms at key points. This is understandable as differentiation is present within the system for two main reasons. One of these is to do with the emotional orientation or characteristics of the people involved in the process and the other is related to the technical nature of the projects themselves, which are often complex and demand input from a number of skills to tasks that have to be combined to produce the completed project.

DECISIONS AND THEIR EFFECT ON STRUCTURE

As referred to in the last chapter, the decision-making process and specifically the timing of decisions made by the client can have a significant influence on the effectiveness of the project organisation. The decisions the client makes will be based upon recommendations or alternatives presented by the project team, usually through its manager. Such decision points act as 'pinch points' through which the project must pass if it is to progress. If an acceptable decision cannot be made, the project will not squeeze through the 'pinch points' and will terminate, or the objectives will be revised. Between these major decision points will be others at which decisions will not normally be made by the client but by the project team manager, depending upon the authority pattern that has been established.

Decisions taken at the project team level will contribute to those taken by the client and at each level the manager of the project team needs to integrate the various tasks to produce the alternative propositions available. The manager will then make the decision when it is within his authority or make a recommendation to the client if the latter is to make the decision. In order to stand the best chance of making the correct decision, the range of available alternatives and supporting arguments will have to be presented in each case. It is the manager's role to make sure that all the alternatives are exposed and to achieve this he will have to take account of the advice of all the contributors to the project. Integration of the contributors therefore assumes paramount importance. The integration of contributors within and between tasks is important, but the key integrating activity of the manager is in bringing together the output of the tasks in a way that allows the range of available alternatives to be clearly exposed.

Thus the essential determinant of the structure of an organisation for the design and construction of a project is the arrangement of decision points and the way in which the contributors need to be integrated in order to produce the material upon which decisions can be made. The most significant decisions are taken by the client and the timing and sequence of the decision points will be determined by the internal organisation and external environment of the client's organisation. This framework needs to be elicited by the manager of the project team from the client before he can determine the positions of the decision points for decisions within his authority. The manager will then be in a position to design the integration of the contributors in the project organisation for the purpose of both classes of decision. Whereas it may be possible to identify a list of routine decisions that are common to all construction projects, it is not possible to determine when they will need to be taken until the framework of the client's decision points is known. Nor is it possible to identify non-routine decisions within the authority of the manager until the client's decision framework is established. Given knowledge of that and of its level of certainty, the manager is able to integrate his decisions and the contribution of his team in the most effective manner.

A major task of the manager of the project will therefore be to make the client realise the fundamental nature of his role in the construction process and the way in which it can affect its effectiveness and his own satisfaction with the project outcome.

DIFFERENTIATION AND INTEGRATION IN PRACTICE

Differentiation and attempts to integrate are expressed in a whole variety of ways in practice. Experience on one project with a particular group of participants is not necessarily transferable, either to another project or to another group of participants. Each project should be analysed individually to identify the type and scale of differentiation as a basis for designing the appropriate organisation structure and integrating mechanism. Later chapters will examine how this may be achieved but at this point it may be useful to look at some of the problems and solutions which have been commonly tried in practice.

The most positive approach has been the creation of multidisciplinary practices that employ within the one firm all the professional skills associated with projects. If, within such practices, specialists work in project-dedicated teams, then one would expect that conditions would be created in which a high level of integration could occur. However, if such practices continue to organise in 'departments' of specialist skills, a great integrating opportunity will have been lost. In either case, integration with the contractor will be difficult to achieve if he is not appointed until after design has been substantially completed. Even if he is appointed early in the process, differentiation will be high and special integrating effort will be required. A similar situation will exist on a development project if, as often occurs, a general practice (valuation) surveyor is involved from outside the consortium.

Differentiation is high on a project when professional consultants are from separate firms and they will be differentiated from the contractor to varying degrees depending upon when and how he is appointed. If positive attempts are not made to integrate them, the effect upon the project outcome can be serious. A recent example encountered was a project for which the quantity surveyor and services engineer never met but communicated by post and telephone. The result was that the services installation cost control was badly managed, leading to abortive work and dissatisfaction by the client. A more positive approach was discovered on another project on which the professional consultants, although from separate practices, worked together for the whole of the design phase in the office of the consulting engineer who also provided the project management service. At first the consultants did not like the idea of uprooting themselves and working in unfamiliar surroundings but after the event they agreed that it had been very beneficial in creating a harmonious team and producing a project that met the client's requirements.

The familiarity of the contributors with each other's methods as a result of working together on previous projects does, of course, assist integration but can lead to complacency. This can be evident where the same team works on a subsequent project, which places different demands upon the team as a result of the client's requirements and the environmental influences acting upon the process. There is a danger that there may be no stimulant within the team for a change of approach.

As mentioned previously, the problem of integrating the contractor is always present. Many of the new initiatives of contractor involvement in the design team are intended to try to assist the integration of the contractor into the project team. Design-and-build, management contracting, the U.S.A. construction management approach and 'alternative methods of management' are examples of initiatives that bring the designing and constructing functions closer together. Although the benefit claimed for these approaches is that they allow an input of construction knowledge to the design, there is a potential for an equally important benefit in terms of integrating the people working on the project. However, it has yet to be shown whether this is the case in practice.

The appointment of a project manager to a project should act basically as an integrating device although the benefit of such an appointment is often justified in other terms, such as progress chaser, controller, etc. or even just as a preoccupation with titles. One would expect that the greater the differentiation between the contributors, the greater the need for a project manager. The latent differentiation of contributors to all projects as a result of sentience and other forces means that the need for integrating effort is always high and would probably benefit from the integrative effort provided by someone solely concerned with project management.

Most building projects require someone to act as a catalyst. This need is often recognised for large complex projects and there is no doubt that the scale and complexity of such projects, both technically and environmentally, expose differentiation and demand an integrating mechanism such as a project manager. However, the extent of differentiation on the medium sized or even the smaller projects is not as readily recognised but is sufficient to require positive action to integrate the contributors rather than just hoping that it will happen.

International projects can generate the greatest levels of differentiation. Not only will the contributors be differentiated for the reasons given previously, but such differentiation will be compounded by the contributors coming from a variety of countries and being required to apply their skills in a country with which they may not be very familiar. The differences in cultural background and methods of working will generate differentiation, which can only be integrated by careful organisation design and very positive effort. It is therefore not surprising that project managers are employed more frequently on international projects than on national ones. This need is also reinforced on overseas projects by the environmental and often technical complexity of the work, as projects are frequently undertaken to build whole industries and extensive facilities from scratch in conditions of great uncertainty.

Theoretically, to reduce differentiation to a minimum, a client would develop his project using a team of specialist skills as employees within his own organisation ('in house') including the construction phase using directly employed labour. In such a situation the likelihood of conflicting objectives among the contributors would be reduced. The allegiance of the contributors should be largely to the client directly, although allegiance to professional skills would not be eliminated altogether. In this type of arrangement the opportunity to generate the maximum level of integration using an in-house project manager who would have access to and a full understanding of his organisation's objectives should be at its greatest. However, in most cases this is just not practicable as most clients do not have such an in-house capability. Local authority direct labour organisations in the U.K. are one of the few examples of this type of arrangement but their history is not generally one of great success, although there are some successful examples. Perhaps their problem is more political than management orientated. Nevertheless, the in-house scenario is an interesting one upon which to base thinking about the type and degree of differentiation and integration present in any specific project organisation.

MANAGEMENT TECHNIQUES AND PROJECT INFORMATION

Recent years have seen the development of a range of techniques aimed at making the management of construction projects more effective and at providing clients with the means to make more rational and objective decisions. This has been accompanied by the rapid growth of cheap computing power useful to such techniques. However, there is often a gulf between the availability of the array of tools for project control and their actual use on real projects. The opportunity and will to apply techniques depend upon a receptive management structure and an appropriate configuration of contributors to a project. Ability to organise to take advantage of the growth in techniques and computing power has fallen behind the rate of development of technology. This is particularly so for construction projects for which organisational structures are predominantly conventional and reflect the juxtaposition of traditional professional roles. This tends to inhibit innovation with the result that the industry and professions are slower than many other industries in applying new ideas and techniques. How often are techniques such as networking, life cycle cost planning or even cash flow forecasting actually instigated and implemented by the professions and industry themselves on behalf of their clients rather than in response to demands by clients?

The major cause of such a lack of initiative is often the fact that there is no person who is solely concerned with the overall management of the construction process. Each contributor is predominantly concerned with his particular part of the process and is therefore unlikely to generate the use of techniques that have implications for the project as a whole. Traditionally, the architect has overall responsibility for management as well as for design and monitoring of construction, but the architect's allegiance to architecture tends to make him place his overall project responsibilities at a lower priority than architectural matters. In addition, architectural education does not generally equip him with the necessary perspectives for such a role.

A person charged with the sole task of project control is likely to recognise a need for project control techniques and to evaluate and implement those techniques that will help him in the task of overall management of a project. An organisation structure that provides this mechanism should itself initiate the implementation of innovative techniques rather than solely responding to client pressure. A shift in perception from a focus on the parts of the construction process carried out by the specialist contributors to an overview of the process as a whole will not only improve service to clients and the effectiveness of the process but will also raise the reputation and status of the industry and its professions.

The techniques and skills used in the construction process rely fundamentally upon the nature and quality of the information they use and the manner in which the information is structured to make it appropriate and accessible to each particular activity of the project organisation. The co-ordination of project information has been the subject of much research attention in the U.K. and elsewhere but progress in implementing an acceptable co-ordinated universal information system has been slow. Major reasons for this can be found in the points made previously about the implementation of techniques, the temporary nature of most project organisations and the lack of a sufficiently strong lobby of influential people who could be expected to initiate a more structured and acceptable information system.

Information produced during the construction process at present relates to the specific needs of the information generator rather than being useful to the process as a whole. The architect produces drawings and specifications which are themselves often uncoordinated; the engineers do the same and their drawings are often not co-ordinated with those of the architect. The quantity surveyor translates this information into cost plans and bills of quantities, which are again often not co-ordinated between themselves or with the drawings from which they were derived. The contractor uses the bills to tender, and then has to translate the information given in the bills and on the drawings, etc. into a form suitable for use in construction. None of these data are usually co-ordinated with programming and cash flow information.

What is needed is an information system in which the data are transposable between contributors rather than needing to be translated. This would require a fundamental rethink of the way in which information is classified, structured, co-ordinated and prepared. Many standard procedures and conventions, such as standard forms of contract, measurement, etc., impose situations in which the information produced is limited to use for a specific purpose only. If such information were structured as part of an information system in such a way as to be accessible and useful to all project participants, they would not need to translate it laboriously for their own purposes.

An information system should not inhibit or constrain the choice of project organisation structure. If an agreed lowest common denominator of project information could be found, it would allow the various users to build up or rearrange the basic information into the form required and enable it to be co-ordinated with project information generated by others. Any such information system should be subservient to the project organisation system and should recognise that the design process is analytical and the construction process synthetic.

Theoretically, the design process has all the information available to it. It is conceptual at the early stages of the project, which is described in terms of its perceived final form to provide the conditions appropriate for the various user activities to be carried out within it. The design is implicative of resources which are more closely defined as the design develops. The construction process synthesises the resources determined by the design solution to produce the completed building. An information system should reflect this process of design and construction.

The project organisation therefore has all general information available to it at the beginning of the project as input to the transformation system. The project organisation transforms this information into project-specific information in realising the project. If the information gathered and transformed specifically for a project is co-ordinated, it will be available consistently for appraisal of a project at the various stages of its development against a range of criteria for specific needs, e.g. spatial, energy consumption, aesthetics and buildability. Additional information arising from such appraisals should be added to and co-ordinated with the project information as illustrated in fig. 5.1. Therefore each component of the organisation structure should be able to access the information system, use the information and return its results to the co-ordinated system. These ideas may appear rather grandiose but are within the realms of possibility given the computing power now available and the developments taking place in information technology.

The responsibility for designing and implementing an information system for a project rests with the person responsible for managing that project for the client. A more positive approach to project management and project organisation design could lead to a greater use of management techniques and to the design and adoption of project information systems that contribute to effective, co-ordinated communication between participants and provide the data to make management techniques more viable and helpful.

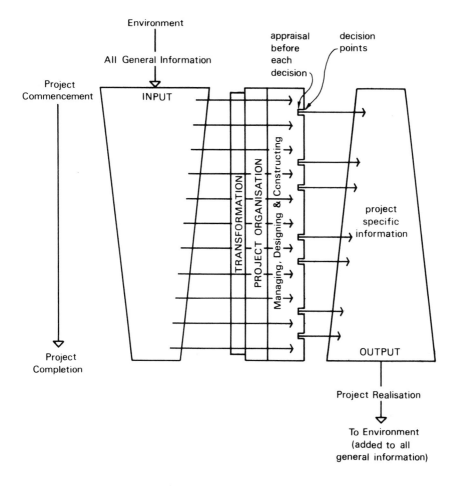

Fig. 5.1   Transformation of information, (with acknowledgement to David M. Jaggar).

REFERENCES

1. Lawrence, P.C. and Lorsch, J.W. (1967) *Organisation and Environment: Managing Differentiation and Integration.* Harvard: Harvard Business.
2. Miller, E.J. and Rice, A.K. (1967) *Systems of Organisation: the Control of Task and Sentient Boundaries.* London: Tavistock Publications.
3. Thompson, J. (1967) *Organisation in Action.* New York: McGraw-Hill.

6 A Model of the Construction Process

INTRODUCTION

It will be useful at this point to draw together the threads that have been running through the previous chapters into a model of the construction process. This approach formalises the ideas that underpin the way in which construction project organisations should be structured and provides an approach to analysing and designing project management structures. Although the approach may at first appear theoretical, it does provide the basis of a practical, analytical tool for examining the effectiveness of the project management process, as described in chapter 9.

The construction process has few fundamental characteristics common to all projects. This is not unexpected in view of the diversity of construction projects and their clients. That being the case, it is necessary to identify those aspects that can be generalised so that they may be interpreted for each individual project. The application of the model will then identify the structure of the process in such a way that it is possible to analyse how it operates in practice.

Such a model may be employed as a tool for learning from experience in a more rigorous way than has been the case in the past, by using it to analyse completed projects. It can also be used for designing organisation structures with the aim of providing the structure which should give the best chance of a successful project outcome as far as the organisational aspects are concerned. The tasks and roles of project management can then be identified on the basis of the organisational structure designed for each specific project. Project success is, of course, dependent upon much more than solely organisational issues,[1] such as behavioural, political and other forces acting upon the project, but if the organisation structure is as well designed as possible, at least the project is off to a good start.

COMMON CHARACTERISTICS

A prerequisite of the model is an outline of the process of providing a project devoid of artificial organisation boundaries such as those created by the conventional and other predetermined approaches to project organisation. Such a model would identify the major forces that influence the process and the fundamental structure that results.

The process has a start point (which may be difficult to identify specifically in practice). It also has a finish point, which is taken as the completion of a project. The process of identifying and providing a project consists of those events that join these two points. Potential start points are activated by organisations which *may* become clients of the construction industry if the process identifies that a construction project is required to meet the objectives of the potential client. The term 'client' is used to refer to a sponsor of construction work who can generate the finance, information and authority necessary to embark upon the process.

Construction projects start as a result of the influence of environmental stimuli upon prospective client organisations which create the motivation and need or opportunity to construct to reach objectives. Such stimuli may be economic, technological, sociological etc. and usually consist of combinations of different classes of forces. The basic response of an organisation to environmental stimuli is the result of its need to survive; above this level the organisation responds in order to expand as the result of its motivation (see fig. 6.1). Survival is the basic goal which requires the organisation to maintain its position relative to those of its competitors for which it must continue to obtain a return acceptable to its environment in terms of its role (e.g. profit, service, acceptability). This is more easily conceived for commercial organisations, but is also true for public authorities.

Expansion is a response to environmental forces by the organisation to take advantage of events in its environment. The degree to which the organisation takes such opportunities is determined by its motivation, which is, in turn, influenced by incentives provided by the environment, e.g. taxation, status, satisfaction. The start point of the process is, therefore, the recognition by the potential client of the need or opportunity to achieve a particular objective for his organisation. The options available to achieve the objective *may* include the acquisition of real property which, in turn, *may* require the construction of a new building, but at this early stage this will not have been established.

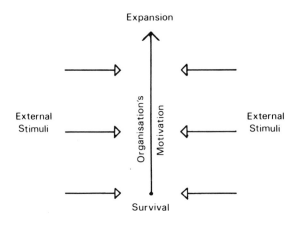

Fig. 6.1   Organisation's response to external influences.

At the initial activation of a start point, the plane within which a finish point is feasible will be very wide and will encompass all those alternatives that allow the organisation to achieve its objective. The alternatives available will vary, depending upon the nature of the organisation's role. For instance, there will be basic differences between the choices available to commercial and public authorities. However, *it is possible*, for every category, that one of the alternatives will require the acquisition of real property.

This outline of the process is now illustrated further using as an example the identification and provision of a project for a commercial organisation. The concepts are more readily understood in terms of commercial criteria, although the same process should be followed by any potential client.

After starting the process, the initial decision of relevance to the construction process is whether or not real property is required. This may be called the *project conception process*, as illustrated in fig. 6.2. If a decision is reached that does not require the construction of a project, then the organisation which was a potential client of the construction industry will not become a client. During this phase, environmental influences are transmitted to the potential client through his importation of information, energy and materials from the environment. The meaning of information and material is self-evident, although it should be pointed out that material encompasses any material whatsoever. Energy similarly means any type of

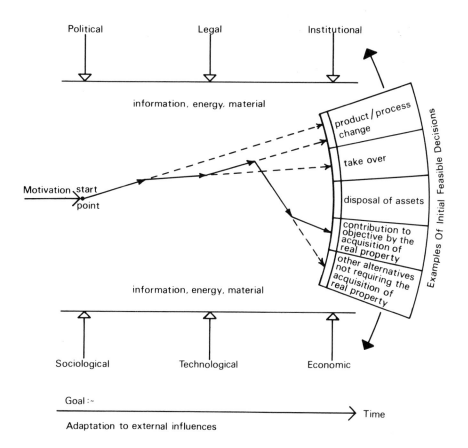

Political   Legal   Institutional

information, energy, material

product / process change

take over

disposal of assets

contribution to objective by the acquisition of real property

other alternatives not requiring the acquisition of real property

Examples Of Initial Feasible Decisions

Motivation start point

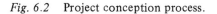

information, energy, material

Sociological   Technological   Economic

Goal :-

→ Time

Adaptation to external influences

Fig. 6.2   Project conception process.

energy, but in this context people are a particularly important source of both physical and mental energy. Such influences can be broadly classified as political, legal, economic, institutional, sociological and technical. The action of these influences will determine the initial decision. The project conception process will entail the consideration of each alternative within the environmental context and a decision will be made on the basis of the influence of the external factors. For example, economic conditions may make a process change appropriate, but it may then be discovered that trade union action (sociological influence) will make this difficult, by which time economic conditions may have made the take-over of another firm more appropriate. This process is one of adapting the client organisation to environmental influences until an initial feasible decision is reached and normally takes place within the client organisation.

In developing the model, it is assumed that the preferred outcome of the project conception stage requires the acquisition of real property to contribute to the satisfaction of the potential client's objective. At this stage, acquisition of real property includes existing or new property or improvement or modification of property already owned.

The assumed preferred decision of the project conception process, which requires the acquisition of real property, contains a number of alternatives which can be considered as an intermediate feasible decision point. The process of arriving at one of these alternatives in making further progress towards the finish point may be called the *project inception process,* and is illustrated in fig. 6.3. The intermediate feasible decision actually made is again determined by the ability of the alternative chosen to contribute to the achievement of the objective of what is now a client of the construction process. The environmental influences acting upon the process of reaching an intermediate decision are the same as those given before, but may exert different influences during this process. The project inception process will receive information, energy and material from the environment and will transform them in its task of identifying the appropriate intermediate decision. Interacting with these influences in arriving at a decision will be the commercial activity of the client, which will itself be influenced by the external factors. For example, the environmental factors affecting the decision will be the state of the property market regarding the availability of existing premises and rent levels, the cost of new building work, site availability, the rate of technological change which determines whether a short-term lease is better than a freehold building, etc.

In developing the model further, it is assumed that the preferred outcome of the project inception process is the construction of a new building. The performance of the building that is actually constructed will lie within a finish spectrum ranging from total satisfaction with performance requirement to total dissatisfaction. The process of arriving at the finished building is called the *project realisation process*, as illustrated in fig. 6.4. This will again be determined by the environmental influences acting on the process. These are classified as before, and again provide information, energy and

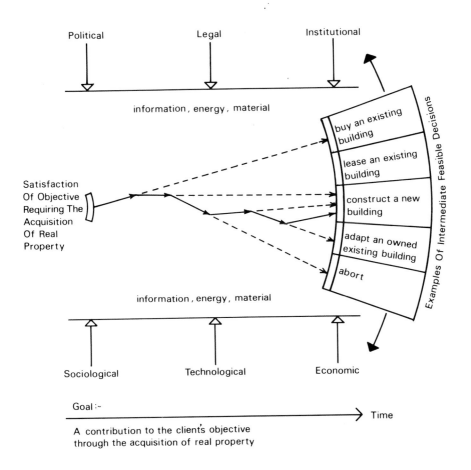

Fig. 6.3   Project inception process.

material for the process. For example, the environment provides the skills, both professional and constructional, which are available to the project. It also determines the availability of materials, and even the weather, which might affect the completion time for the building. The client's environment will affect the certainty of what he requires of the building. If it creates uncertainty, this might generate changes to the design and construction which can affect the cost and completion time for the project. As was the case with the project conception and inception processes, the external influences

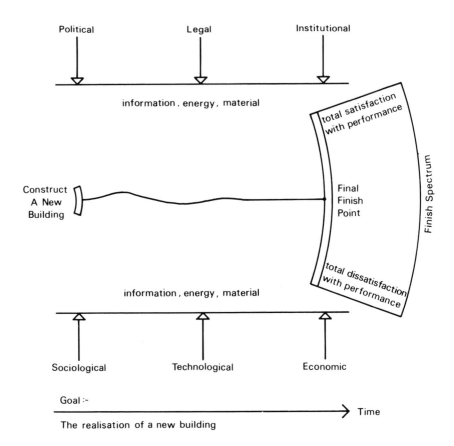

Fig. 6.4   Project realisation process.

act in two ways: directly upon the process and indirectly through their influence upon the commercial activity of the client. The project realisation process transforms these inputs into the output of the process, which is the finished building. The effectiveness of the transformation process will determine the quality of the outcome actually achieved.

A further example of the effect of external influences during this process could be that economic and/or institutional forces determine that construction work is awarded on the basis of a competitive tender. Such a decision would divide this process into two sequential sub-processes, design and construction, but only if appropriate external influences are present. Such an assumption would be unfounded at this stage of development of the outline of the process.

To summarise, there are only three sub-systems that have universal application to all building projects: the project conception, project inception and project realisation sub-systems. These sub-systems generate two primary decision points, one which contains the potential decision that real property is required and, if such a decision is taken, the second decision as to the nature of the real property to be provided. Both these decisions will be taken by the client organisation.

The start point represents the beginning of the project management process and it can be seen that this will, in most cases, be contained and managed within the client organisation during the project conception sub-system. Ideally, the client organisation should, during this process, receive advice from the project team, but in reality this rarely happens. If it were to occur, then the members of the construction team involved would be part of the project management process but would not be leading it, as at this stage a business decision rather than a construction decision is required. However, it would certainly be advantageous for clients to have an input of advice from certain members of the construction team at this stage to enable them to take a fully informed decision.

The project inception sub-system demands a significant input from the project team and the process will require a property- or construction-orientated management system working in conjunction with the client to identify the most appropriate solution to the client's needs. However, project management does not usually take place in this form in practice. It tends to occur implicitly, solely within the client organisation, and project teams are often faced with a *fait accompli* by the client. They can, therefore, often do little other than proceed on the basis of the client's preconceived idea of the best solution to his problem. It would be advantageous to both the client, in terms of the utility of the completed building, and the project team, through their increased effectiveness, if clients were to involve members of the project team in this process.

The project realisation sub-system is the process that is most readily perceived by clients and project teams as that in which project management takes place, although even in this process it is sometimes construed as being concerned only with the construction phase rather than with the whole process, including design. Even though project management may be led by someone from the project team during this process, the management of the process is likely to benefit significantly from the involvement of the client.

As there are only three sub-systems that are universally applicable to construction projects, it is necessary to identify the factors that determine the sub-systems within each of these major sub-systems identified by the primary decisions discussed previously. As most projects differ, the sub-systems required to achieve them will also differ as a result of the task being undertaken and the environment within which it is carried out. Therefore the further sub-systems cannot be defined explicitly, but it is possible to identify the factors that create them, the nature of their relationships and their need for integration.

SUB-SYSTEMS

The primary decision points differentiate the major sub-systems and define the boundaries between them. Similarly, other decision points will determine the boundaries between other sub-systems. The construction process is characterised by a series of decision points. These act as pinch points through which the project must pass if progress is to be made. If the project cannot pass a pinch point, then it will be aborted. Decision points are arranged in a hierarchy of which the primary decision points are at the highest level. Below them occur key decision points and operational decision points.

KEY DECISION POINTS

Further discontinuity in the system is created by key decision points. Key decisions are those that the client will make for himself. They are determined by environmental influences acting upon the client organisation and are often manifest in the client's internal procedures for expenditure and similar approvals. They can range from, for example, approval of design and budget proposals and decisions to delay the project, to decisions to change the nature of the project. Such decisions imply a degree of irrevocability, as to revoke such decisions would entail the client in a loss of resources.

The process of providing a project is characterised by discontinuity created by the need for decisions. As they reflect the flow of the process they are fundamental to the organisation structure of the project. The integrating mechanism provided between the client and the members of the project team is, therefore, highly significant for the success of the project. This mechanism should aim to anticipate key decision points and organise so that decisions can be made on the basis of the contribution of the members of the project team, who have a part to play in providing information and advice on which such decisions should be based. The nature of the client's organisation can have a fundamental influence on the effectiveness of this process. If the client is represented by a committee or board of directors, they will have to decide how they themselves are to take key decisions or whether they will delegate this function to some member of their own organisation and, if so, to what extent they will delegate. Similarly, they will have to decide upon the extent of delegated authority given to the project team as this will determine which are the key decisions. Decisions taken by the project team are classified as *operational decisions.* The greater the number of decisions classified as operational, the greater will be the flexibility available to the project team and the more control they will have over the decision-making process. There is likely to be less uncertainty and delay and more integration, for example, in those cases where a client's representative has sufficient delegated authority to make many key decisions, or in cases where the project team deals directly with, say, a managing director acting with full authority. This is likely to be the situation in the former case only where the client has great confidence in the representative and, in the latter case, for the smaller private company. Very real difficulties can be created for the larger private companies and public authorities if an appropriate integrating mechanism is not or cannot be designed. A common problem is that of key decisions taking longer than anticipated, with a resultant delay to the project, which can often have a corresponding knock-on effect for later project activities. A further common problem is that if the client's organisation is unresponsive to environmental forces and the needs of the construction process, key decision points may be inappropriately identified in terms of the nature of the decision and its timing. An important task of the leader of the project team is, therefore, to endeavour to make clear to the client the team's needs in terms of the timing and quality of key decisions. Yet, at the same time, he must recognise that the project will place heavy demands upon the client's organisation, which will have to continue to carry out its main functions as well as being involved in the design and construction of the project.

Key decisions lie beneath the primary decisions in the decision hierarchy and, therefore, contribute to them. Until a primary decision point is reached and the decision is taken, key decisions will be cumulative. They therefore provide major feedback opportunities for both the client and the project team. Each key decision should be checked against the overall objective of the project and the primary and key decisions already taken, to ensure that the project is remaining on course. If it is not, then it will either have to be returned to course or the original objectives or previous decisions will have to be reassessed to establish whether the deviation is beneficial and feasible. Whereas the primary decisions create the boundaries between the major systems of the process, the key decisions represent the boundaries between the main sub-systems which constitute the major systems and provide feedback opportunities as shown in fig. 6.5.

OPERATIONAL DECISION POINTS

In bringing forward propositions upon which key decisions will be based, the members of the project team will themselves have to make decisions based upon their professional and technical competence. These will not affect the policy of the client's organisation: such decisions will be primary and key, and will be taken by the client. Therefore the decisions taken by the project team in making progress towards a key decision are described as operational. The range of propositions that may be presented to a client, and the operational decisions implicit in defining the propositions, will be the responsibility of the leader of the project team. The leader will also have the responsibility for integrating his team to ensure that all relevant advice has been given before arriving at an operational decision. He must also make certain that the full range of propositions appropriate to the client's objectives have been formulated and that they are presented objectively.

In practice, on many projects clients are not presented with alternative propositions and in such cases operational decisions are made to move the process towards the next key decision point. As with the latter, operational decision points will also represent 'pinch points' through which the project must pass if progress is to be made. Although they do not have the same degree of irrevocability and associated loss of resources as key decisions, nevertheless operational decisions which are later changed are likely to cause delay and some

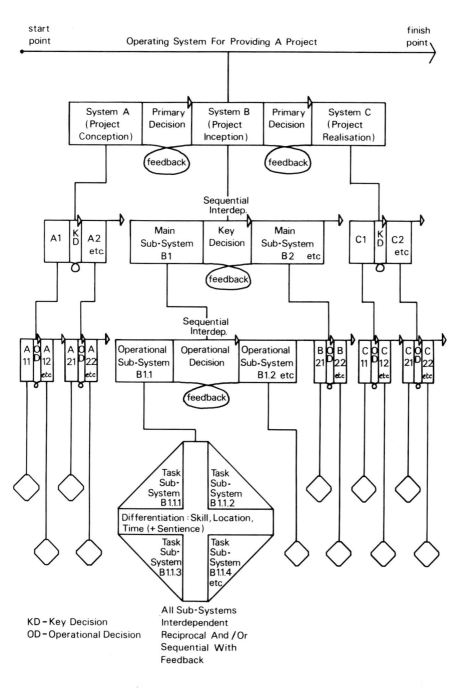

Fig. 6.5 The operating system.

loss of resources. Examples of operational decisions include the details of project programmes, the use of bills of quantities for tender documentation, and alternative design proposals. These decisions are therefore mainly concerned with technical and pro-fessional decisions and with the implementation of procedural aspects of projects, and move the project incrementally towards a key decision. Their position in the system will be determined by previously taken key decisions, but there will be more opportunity for the project team to design the structure of these decision points than is the case with key decision points.

Operational decision points present secondary feedback oppor-tunities. Each time an operational decision is being considered, it should be checked against the previous operational decisions within the sub-system and against the last key decision to ensure that it is compatible with what has been decided previously. If it is incom-patible, opportunity to change the decision exists or, alternatively, to amend a previous operational or key decision, although this is unlikely to be the outcome at an operational decision point.

Each sub-system created by key decisions will, therefore, consist of a number of operational sub-systems, as illustrated in fig. 6.5. The number of sub-systems created by key decisions and operational decisions cannot be prescribed for all projects as they will vary considerably in both number and nature depending upon the type of project required and the environmental conditions in which it is to be achieved. However, the model does provide a basis for identifying them for individual projects.

TASK SUB-SYSTEMS

In arriving at an operational decision, each operational sub-system will consist of at least one task sub-system. The task sub-system level is where the contributors to the project work together to bring forward the propositions upon which operational decisions are based. At operational and key decision level it will be the job of the manager of the process from both the client's organisation and the project team to bring together the decisions in a manner compatible with the client's objectives.

The following illustrates the task sub-system level for an oper-ational sub-system concerned with 'identifying a site' at the same time as which the outline requirements of the client are being finalised and feasibility studies also have to be carried out.

This would require three task sub-systems to be operating with reciprocal interdependency. Various people would be carrying out the three tasks and taking advice from a range of different people. For instance, the managing director of the client organisation could be finalising his outline requirements with advice from his departmental managers and, perhaps, some representatives of the project team; a commercial property agent could be trying to identify a suitable site with advice, say, from the managing director, architect and quantity surveyor; and the feasibility studies would be carried out by the quantity surveyor with advice from the property agent, architect, structural engineer and managing director. The result of this interaction should be propositions which could result in an operational decision to enter negotiations for a site prior to a key decision to purchase. The problem of managing this type of process is one of integrating such a diverse range of interdependent contributors. In modelling this element in generalised terms, therefore, it is necessary to identify the features that generate the differentiation requiring integration.

The determinants of differentiation have been expressed by Miller[2] as technology, territory and time and have general relevance to the construction process. The idea of differentiation, as described in the last chapter, provides the tools for analysing different situations that give rise to various levels of differentiation and hence to the need for matching levels of integration. An understanding of the degree of differentiation present in a system significantly aids the person managing the system to provide the appropriate level and mechanisms of integration.

Separation of people working together on a project is affected by the skills (*technology*) they bring to bear on the project. People from different skill backgrounds (e.g. architect, engineer, quantity surveyor, builder) work on problems in different ways, which stem from their experience, and they often cannot see the other contributors' points of view. Such conflicts need reconciling by the manager of the system in terms of the client's objectives. Similarly, separation on the basis of location (*territory*) creates boundaries between contributors. Territory refers to the geographical distance between groups of people working on the project and this obviously affects communication to a very large extent. Often, signboards on building sites will show that the firms contributing to a project are located many miles apart. How much easier it is to resolve a problem on a project through face-to-face discussion rather than by telephone or letter. The advantages to be gained through the contributors working together in the same office (although from different firms), particularly during design, are likely to be significant. A further differentiator is *time*. Although this was visualised by Miller in relation to shift working, it is relevant to the contributors to construction projects in terms of the sequence of activities to be performed where a particular contributor cannot perform his activity until another has completed his.

Overlying and reinforcing differentiation on the basis of the above is sentience, also referred to in the last chapter. It is a particularly strong force in the construction industry and gives rise to strong allegiances to a profession or a firm or to both.

Figure 6.5 illustrates that each operational sub-system will consist of task sub-systems and the people working within them will be differentiated on the basis of skill, location and time, reinforced by sentience. The number and nature of the task sub-systems and the people working within them have to be defined for each individual project as they will vary significantly.

THE OPERATING SYSTEM AND THE MANAGING SYSTEM

What has been defined so far in the model is the operating system - that system of activity through which the project is achieved. Figures 6.2 to 6.5 model, in abstract terms, the generality of the construction process. The operating system is managed by a managing system, which carries out the decision-making, maintenance and regulatory activities that keep the operating system going. It is differentiated on the basis of skill from the operating system. The skill of the managing system is management and those of the operating system are professional and technical. The managing system referred to here is that which acts on behalf of the client. It is concerned with the totality of the process of providing the project, which includes that part of the client's organisation relevant to the process. Each system and sub-system into which the process is differentiated may have its own managing system, but such systems will not be managing the total system for the client.

The actual form which the managing system takes in practice will vary considerably. It may be contained solely within the client's organisation, where the client has this capability; in other cases it may consist of a client's representative and a 'consultant' project manager. In the conventional arrangement of contributors it would be the architect acting in a dual role of manager and designer. Alternatively, it may be undertaken by a variety of people at different stages of the project.

The managing system controls the boundaries between the systems and sub-systems and integrates their output to ensure that the primary and key decisions made at these boundaries are compatible with the client's requirements. The managing system should ensure that boundaries are appropriately drawn in relation to the process, that facilities for appropriate feedback are available and are used, and that the correct decisions are taken. To achieve this, the managing system also seeks to control the boundaries between the process and its environment, and between the process and the client and his environment.

In order to support this role, the managing system needs to monitor the performance of the systems and sub-systems. Such intra-system regulatory activities are intended to ensure that the manner by which systems and sub-systems arrive at the propositions upon which decisions are based is appropriate. This entails the design and use of feedback mechanisms and requires the managing system to integrate the sub-systems and to ensure that appropriate techniques are used. Although monitoring activities will also be carried out by the systems' and sub-systems' own managers, nevertheless the managing system of the total process acting for the client will need to convince itself that the operating system is using appropriate methods.

The managing system also needs to ensure that the resources that produce the output of the systems and sub-systems (for example, and in particular, people) are procured and replenished. These activities aim to ensure that the operating system has the capacity both quantitatively and qualitatively to perform its tasks. Such activities will also be carried out by the managers of the systems and sub-systems, but the managing system of the total process acting for the client will again need to determine the fact that the operating system has the capacity to perform its tasks.

DESIGN OF ORGANISATION STRUCTURES

The ability of a managing system to operate effectively depends upon an appropriately structured operating system and complimentary managing system. The model has identified, in systems terms, the elements of importance in structuring organisations and has attempted to relate them, in abstract terms, to the construction process. It does not, therefore, present a rigid proposition for the organisation structure of the construction process, but proposes an approach that responds to the specific demands of individual projects. A role of the managing system is to design the organisation through which it will work in seeking to achieve the client's objectives. The manager must, therefore, be provided with the authority to design the operating and managing systems and to make them function. Such authority will stem from the client, who must decide the pattern of authority established for the project.

Against the background of the model, and accepting that the client's objectives will have been spelled out, an approach to designing an organisation structure for a building project could be:

(a)   The manager convinces the client of the need to design an organisation structure for both the construction process and for his own organisation's relationship with it, and makes the client aware of the demands that will be placed upon his organisation.

(b)   The project organisation structure is designed at the very beginning of the process.

(c)   Primary decision points are identified.

(d)   Within each system created by the primary decision points, the key decision points are anticipated as far as possible.

(e)   Within each main sub-system created by the key decision points, operational decision points are identified.

(f)   Feedback loops are established within the structure produced by (c), (d) and (e).

(g)   The task sub-systems within the operational sub-systems are identified, together with the skills required to undertake them.

(h)   The manner by which the skills are to be provided is established, e.g. separate specialist firms, design-and-build, etc.

(i)   Methods of achieving the required level of integration needed because of the differentiation generated by the system are established, including methods of integrating the client.

(j)   The pattern of managing system activities is identified as a product of the structure of the operating system and the manner by which skills are provided. This would include the authority and responsibility pattern of the managing system, the client and the contributors to the operating system.

(k) Methods of monitoring, mitigating and harnessing the effects of environmental forces are identified.

The extent to which this approach can be achieved in practice will depend upon the relative certainty of the climate in which the project is being undertaken. With a high level of uncertainty, it may be that the organisation can be designed only a stage at a time, but by going through the process suggested, areas of uncertainty will be recognised. For projects with more stable environments, the organisation structure will be easier to lay down and should present a sound basis for close control of the project.

The essence of the approach is that one starts with a statement of what is to be accomplished through identification of the decision points in the process. This is then followed by the design of an operating system required to undertake the tasks prior to each decision, and only then is the managing system designed to suit what is to be achieved. Thus, organisation structure design *follows* the process flow rather than the process having to fit into a predetermined operating and managing system.

REFERENCES

1. Churchman, C.W. (1975) 'Towards a Theory of Application in Systems Science' *Proceedings of the I.E.E.E.* Vol. 63 (No. 3).
2. Miller, E.J. (1959) 'Technology, territory and time' *Human Relations* Vol. XII (No. 3).

7 Activities of Project Management

INTRODUCTION

The idea of the managing system as separate from the operating system has been introduced previously. The operating system carries out the professional and technical tasks required for a project and the managing system integrates and controls its work. The process being managed starts with the objectives of the client's organisation and transforms them into the aesthetic, functional, time and price criteria for the proposed project and, ultimately, into the completed project itself which should satisfy those criteria. The managing system undertakes a range of activities and fulfils a number of roles in this process.

The range of activities required to be carried out by the operating system varies between projects, depending upon the nature of the project, its environmental context and the consequent arrangement of decision points. The detailed work of the managing system will also vary but, nevertheless, its activities can be conceived irrespective of the structure of the project. They are therefore first discussed in general terms before introducing the more detailed functions of project management.

Managing activities are exercised over the people carrying out each of the tasks making up the project process but more importantly they are concerned with managing the interrelationships of the tasks (or, put another way, with managing the 'space' between people and between tasks), and with managing the relationship of the project to its environment.

APPROVAL AND RECOMMENDATION

Perhaps the most important relationship within the managing system is the connection between the power of approval and the right to make recommendations. The power of approval is, of course, exercised at the decision points in making decisions. The right to make recommendations refers to the authority to make a specific recommendation or to present the alternatives upon which a decision will be based. A person with this role is in a very influential position to persuade the person with approval powers to make a particular decision and so select the alternative that the person with recommendation powers wants.

The managing system normally consists of at least two components, one representing the client and the other the person managing the project for him. The former will normally be a member of the client's organisation and the latter a member of the project team employed for the specific project. The pattern of approval and recommendation powers between them will depend upon the role the client decides to take and the structure of his organisation. For example, on three recently examined projects, clients reserved for themselves approval of the output of most tasks up to commencement of construction, with the exception of a small number of tasks that did not involve choices between alternatives, e.g. preparing contract documentation. The level at which the approval powers were vested in the client organisation's hierarchy depended upon the structure of his organisation. For example, for one project the early decisions were approved by local directors of the parent company until the basic parameters had been established. Then approval powers passed to the client's in-house project engineer. Subsequently, the directors were only involved in approvals at a limited number of decision points. Then, for the construction phase, approval powers passed to the manager of the project team (who was titled project manager and was employed by the engineering consultants). These powers did not, however, include responsibility for approval of further project instructions and of documentation, including drawings, produced by the design team, which the client's project engineer approved. The project manager had the role of recommending courses of action for the client's approval which included presenting and advising upon the choices available. It was this activity from which he derived his authority on the project. The project manager approved proposals of the contributors, but the final approval to proceed remained with the client.

For two other projects the client's organisational structure was simpler, with the group chairman and managing director respectively representing the client throughout the project; they personally retained approval powers for all decisions during design but not during construction. Again, the manager of the project team recommended actions to the client except during construction, when the manager had approval powers and also had responsibility for approving a small number of routine tasks during design. For these projects additional design information during construction was not subject to approval by the client. The manager of the project again drew his authority from his recommending power.

These arrangements illustrate clients' wishes to be closely associated with their projects and an unwillingness to delegate approval powers. The opportunity for public sector clients to adopt the same position is much more difficult, particularly if the client takes the form of a committee. In this situation the 'client committee' is likely to make one of its officers responsible for managing the project as one of the components of the managing system. This can produce a complex situation regarding approval powers and may result in them being split three ways, part with the 'committee', part with the manager from the client organisation, and part with the manager from the project team.

These issues demonstrate the importance of integration between the client's organisation and the process of construction. It is clear that the client will determine the approval pattern within a project and hence define the authority of his managers of the project. The degree to which this can be formalised will depend upon the will of the client as influenced by the managers. Although it would be ideal to have approval and recommendation powers written down in an explicit form, in reality it is difficult to persuade clients to do this adequately. Nevertheless, it is an ideal for which managers should continue to strive. However, even if it is achieved, there will still remain the problem of interpretation.

The key to these relationships is understanding and communication between the parties involved, which cannot be fully dependent upon formality but which will draw strength from the informal integration of the people concerned through discussion of the issues surrounding the project. In all probability the relationship between approval and recommendation powers will evolve during the project as trust and understanding develop between the participants. Nevertheless, efforts should be made by the client and managers of the project to establish guidelines for these relationships as soon as possible in the project's development.

BOUNDARY CONTROL, MONITORING AND MAINTENANCE

Boundary control, monitoring and maintenance represent the basic project management activities carried out by the managing system. These activities are normally carried out by the component of the managing system drawn from the project team, although if the client's organisation has the capability, they could be carried out by his people.

The objective of boundary control is to ensure functional compatibility of contributors' work within and between tasks, to relate the system to its environment and to control the system's direction towards the required outcome. It is fundamental to the achievement of the level of integration and control demanded by a project and to a satisfactory project outcome. Boundary control derives its name from its role in managing the boundaries between the various subsystems of the project.

This activity is normally accompanied by the complementary activities of monitoring and maintenance. Monitoring is intra-task regulation to check and control prior to output that a task is proceeding in a manner which will achieve its purpose. Maintenance ensures that a task has the capability to achieve that purpose.

Boundary control involves setting up formal control mechanisms using the feedback loops defined by the key and operational decision points identified when designing the organisation structure, and establishing the supporting information system. It ensures that information flows as intended and that feedback mechanisms are activated. In addition, boundary control should ensure that the reciprocal and sequential interdependencies identified in designing the organisation structure are made to work in the manner intended.

Sequential interdependencies can be integrated by ensuring proper information flow in accordance with the information system, but reciprocal interdependencies need to be integrated using mechanisms that ensure that contributors meet in the correct combinations and at the right times. Such mechanisms would normally include action-minuted meetings and exploratory and less formal meetings in the critical early stages of the project. Where contributors are from different firms, it could, and in many cases should, extend to bringing the people together in one place to work on the project rather than their relying on correspondence and telephone communication. These activities include ensuring that the client is integrated in the appropriate manner at the various stages, and keeping in close contact with him to identify any changes in his environment that may affect his requirements. Whereas boundary control relates the parts of the system to each other in the way described earlier, monitoring seeks to ensure that the individuals or groups undertaking a specific task respond to the demands to integrate and also that techniques and procedures appropriate to the specific task are being used.

Maintenance involves keeping in close touch with each contributor and ensuring that each is equipped to carry out the task required of him. It requires regular formal reviews of the quality and quantity of resources dedicated to the project, particularly in relation to the number and level of skill of the people employed on the project.

Boundary control, monitoring and maintenance are managing system activities and, in accordance with the proposition that the managing and operating systems should be differentiated (on the basis of the skills needed), they should be vested in someone who is not also undertaking operating system activities on the project.

These ideas of what the managing system should be doing sit uncomfortably upon the way in which the construction industry and its professions have evolved. They demand a much greater involvement, some may say interference, by the managing system for the project (e.g. by the project manager) in the activities and tasks carried out by the contributors. The evolution of the industry and its professions has resulted in the creation of a large number of independent firms, but they are interdependent when working together on a project. These ideas, therefore, suggest that control over such firms, both in terms of their relationships with each other and, more significantly, in terms of the activities within a firm, are a legitimate activity of the project management process.

If the managing system is to control the construction process satisfactorily, it requires the authority to carry out boundary control, monitoring and maintenance activities in connection with the activities of all the contributors. The contributors would have to be prepared to accept such authority while still remaining responsible for their individual input, whereas the managing system should be responsible for overall project control. This web of formal relationships is one of the most difficult aspects of structuring a project organisation and one which is not readily faced by clients and project teams. The managing system needs to ensure that it is properly worked out, documented and understood by the participants at an early stage in the process.

Notwithstanding the need for structural relationships to be defined, in reality the effectiveness of the project team will depend ultimately upon the informal relationships generated by the managing system. They will be the product of the way in which it deals with the project team in carrying out its boundary control, monitoring and maintenance activities. Its objectives should be to weld the contributors into a true team and to ensure that they recognise that satisfaction of the client's objectives should be synonymous with satisfaction of their own.

GENERAL AND DIRECT OVERSIGHT

There are two further classes of supervision of relevance to the project management level of control, general and direct oversight. Although these are not project management activities as such, the concepts are directly relevant to the effectiveness of the project management process. This does not mean that other managing activities at lower levels in the project hierarchy do not have implications for project management, but they would be the responsibility of the contributing firms and be overseen by the managing system through monitoring and maintenance activities.

General oversight provides policy guidance for the project and *direct oversight* is concerned with directly supervising specific skills used on the project. The manner by which these activities are distributed among the project team depends upon the structure of the firms that contribute to the project organisation. In the case of general oversight (policy guidance), this will often be exercised by the client in the conception process of the project until its broad outlines are approved by him. The actual person appointed to undertake this activity depends upon the structure of the client's organisation. If the client's component of the project managing system is provided by a person in authority in the client's organisation, e.g. the managing director, then he will normally be providing general oversight as well as being part of the managing system. In the early stages of the project, before the project team is involved, he will be guiding other members of his organisation as the ideas for the development of the project are generated. In such a situation he may then also become part of the managing system when the project team becomes involved. On the other hand, if the client is represented by a committee, it will provide general oversight. If,

as is probable, it delegates to a member of its organisation responsibility for managing the project in conjunction with the project
team, the committee will continue to give guidance on policy matters.

A range of possible arrangements are available, and the one selected
will be a function of the client's organisation structure. What is
important is to understand who is exercising which function.

As the project progresses, the policy guidance will probably pass
from the higher management levels of the client's organisation to
lower levels. For example, it may pass from the board of directors
to the client's 'in house' project engineer and result in him being
responsible for general oversight as well as being a component in
the managing system.

Subsequently, general oversight may pass to the project team
when the detailed work on the project commences. The person who
then exercises it depends upon the structure of the firm providing
the management of the project. For example, if this function is
provided by a firm of project managers and the actual project manager is not a partner in his firm, then a partner may provide policy
guidance on behalf of the client. The degree to which general oversight on behalf of the client is exercised by someone in this position
will depend upon the degree to which the client is prepared to
delegate at this stage. If the project manager is also a partner in his
firm, he will probably exercise both general oversight and project
management activities.

A danger at the stage of detailed implementation of the project
arises if the client leaves the project team to 'get on with it'. If the
managing system is not properly structured and consequently the
contributors pursue their work relatively independently, policy
guidance may not be provided and the managing system will not be
structured in such a way that the lack of guidance is recognised.

The manner by which direct oversight is provided again depends
upon the structure of the contributing organisations. Direct oversight
is the highest level of supervision exercised over the individual
skills used on the project, for example by a partner of one of the
contributing professional firms over the activities of his people
working on the project. Similarly, the relationships between direct
supervision and project management depend upon this structure.

For example, where all professional skills and the components
of the managing system from the project team are provided by a
multidisciplinary firm, direct oversight will be provided by the

departmental managers of the firm for each particular skill. Such managers may also be partners of the firm but would not also be acting as project managers if the managing and operating systems are kept separate. Some other member of the firm would be acting as project manager and the relationship between project management and direct oversight should be established within the firm. If the contributors are from separate professional firms, their partners will carry out direct oversight, and the relationship with project management, if also provided by a separate firm, will need to be established and could be potentially more difficult to achieve.

Many other arrangements could exist but, again, the important thing is to recognise where responsibilities lie. In many cases, professionally qualified members of contributing firms do not require direct supervision, but this depends upon their status and the policy of the firm by which they are employed.

Because of the use of competitive tenders for construction work and the consequent standard conditions of contract (e.g. FIDIC), it is difficult for either general or direct supervision of construction work to be provided by the manager of the project for the client or by any of the design team contributors. This responsibility is vested directly in the main contractor and subcontractors. Standard conditions of contract usually cast the architect or other manager in a passive role in connection with the construction work. The contract is directly between the client and the contractor and the rights and duties of both parties to the contract are specified. The architect or project manager is defined as acting to monitor that the conditions of the contract are carried out. They often cannot intervene directly to ensure compliance with the contract but must follow the administrative procedures laid down, with final recourse to arbitration or law by either party to settle disputes.

If dissatisfied with the contractor's performance, and if satisfaction cannot be achieved by persuasion, the manager of the project for the client must recommend legal action to the client as a last resort. More purposeful management of the construction stage on behalf of the client will require forms of contract that differ significantly from those commonly used for competitive bidding. This could result in a consequent redistribution of risk and perhaps a realignment of responsibility for design and a subsequent redefinition of roles, as found, for example, in management contracting.

PATTERN OF ACTIVITIES

The pattern of managing activities on a project will, therefore, be dependent upon the structure of the firms used in the project organisation and upon the client's organisation structure and his requirements regarding the approval powers he wishes to retain. The pattern will also depend to a large extent upon when the client introduces the project team into the process. However, the manager of the project on behalf of the client would normally undertake the activities of boundary control, monitoring and maintenance.

When a project organisation is designed, it is important that the people exercising the various managing activities are identified and their roles understood by all contributors. In this way the authority and responsibilities of the members of the contributing firms will be recognised. For example, it will be known whether the job quantity surveyor has full authority for quantity surveying matters or whether he is subject to direct oversight by a more senior member of his firm. This will depend upon the firm from which he comes and his status within that firm.

The manager of the project team is usually involved in recommending courses of action to the client for approval. His authority does not therefore generally derive from his power to approve the output of contributors but from his power of recommendation, which implies approval of the output, and hence his power to influence decisions made by the client. His authority stems from his access to the client and although this should not bar other contributors from the client if integration of the client is to take place, the latter can vest authority in his manager by considering recommendations only from this source and by requiring other contributors to route recommendations through the manager. Only in this way will the manager have the authority necessary to ensure that the other contributors perform adequately, and have the opportunity to exercise fully his integrating activities. Nevertheless, this situation will only be maintained for any length of time if the manager has the professional respect of the other contributors. The manager of the project may be under general supervision by another person higher in the hierarchy of his firm and this may affect the regard in which he is held by other contributors, at least initially. His authority is likely to be enhanced if he is a partner or director of his firm.

It would be beneficial if the client were to state formally the authority of the manager of the project and of the other contributors.

However, the informal authority of the manager, derived from the respect in which he is held by the client and other contributors, will be the most potent factor and will be the instrument most likely to elicit the necessary level of performance from all contributors.

An example of how activities may be distributed is shown in fig. 7.1. However, as has been stressed, there are many ways in which roles and activities may be distributed, and fig. 7.1 shows in outline only one example.

The allocation of responsibility for the project among the contributors will depend upon the association of firms involved and will be the subject of negotiation between the client and the contributors. However, it is possible to put forward ideas as to how responsibility may be distributed. Conditions of contract for construction work will usually define responsibility for this aspect and the related responsibility of the other contributors in connection with this stage, but they do not have to follow the standard format and can be tailored to suit particular projects. Responsibility for design and associated work is the aspect for which responsibility can be more difficult to define.

If a project is managed and designed by a multidisciplinary practice, then responsibility will rest with that firm. Similarly, responsibilities when a conventional arrangement is used, with the architect as designer/manager, are generally understood. In this arrangement, if the consultants are directly appointed by the client, then they will be responsible to the client for their own work. The difficulties that arise in this respect result from the interrelationship of the contributions made and hence from the allocation of final responsibility for specific deficiencies.

If management of the project for the client is given to a firm separate from the firms making up the operating system, a comparable situation will arise if they are appointed directly by the client. Alternatively, if the project is managed by a firm which appoints the consultants directly, i.e. as 'subcontractors' to them, then the managing firm will take responsibility for their work and hence the total project. If a legal action is successfully brought against them by a client, they may have recourse against their 'subcontractors'. This argument can be extended to design-and-build contracts in which one firm will be responsible for the whole of the design and construction of a project.

Naturally, the greater the responsibility accepted by a firm the

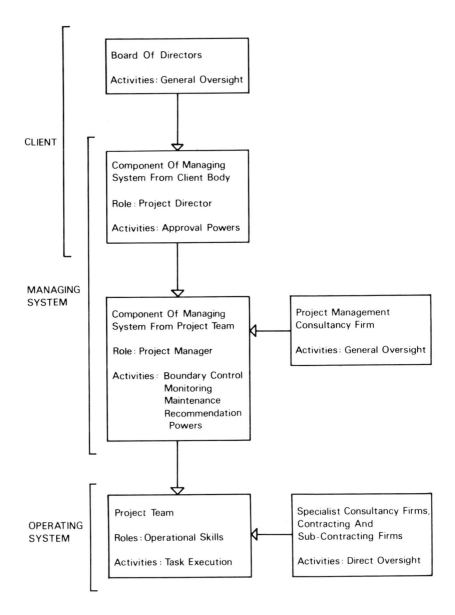

Fig. 7.1 An example of how roles and activities may be distributed.

greater is the risk they are carrying. Firms, whether managing or design-and-build, are unlikely to accept higher responsibility unless they have direct control over the contributors through direct employment, or a facility to bring an action against a contributor if one is brought against them by the client. Importantly, their profit margin would have to be sufficiently high to allow for the level of risk being accepted.

A situation in which responsibility for the project rests with only one firm, or at least one firm for management, design and related aspects and one firm for construction, is likely to be attractive to clients. Informed clients are in a position to dictate the pattern that they want for their project although the reaction of the contributors is likely to be to wish to spread responsibility unless they are appropriately recompensed for risk. Ideally, responsibility should be matched by authority, but this is particularly difficult to achieve. The responsibility pattern adopted should reflect the project structure and the approval and recommendation pattern required by the client. It also should provide the client with legal protection that is sufficiently practical to be applied.

FUNCTIONS OF PROJECT MANAGEMENT

The abstract account of the activities of project management given previously needs interpreting into the functions that should be expected from project management. In undertaking this, concentration is placed upon project management carried out by the manager of the project team rather than by the client's component of the managing system. This is not to minimise the management of the project that takes place within the client's organisation. It is fundamental to the success of the project and provides the context which to a large extent determines how effective the project team can be.

The client should involve the project team at as early a stage as possible and, prior to involving them, should bring forward his initial need for the project in a co-ordinated and controlled way from within his organisation. This requires the client to have taken all useful advice from within his organisation before bringing forward for the project team's advice the strategies that he believes will fulfil his objectives. The client should not have too rigid ideas at this stage as advice from the project team could lead to a better solution to his problem. It would be advantageous if the person who has co-ordinated the client's work and brought forward the strategies could form the client's component of the managing system when the project team is introduced.

The way in which the client carries out this process will be determined by the structure of his organisation but it is important that it should be made explicit to the person from the project team who forms their component of the managing system (referred to in what follows as the project manager). As mentioned previously, the person managing the project team for the client does not have to carry the title of project manager and it may be the architect or engineer who is responsible for managing the process; however, the term is used for convenience.

Consequently, the functions of project management that are discussed here are those that follow from this point and are carried out by the project manager. The detailed functions identified will not necessarily be performed on every project but are intended to illustrate the breadth of project management functions that may be required. Many of them will be repeated in finer degrees of detail at the different stages of the project as further information becomes available. They have not therefore been allocated to the major systems of the process, but require interpretation by the project manager in the light of their degree of applicability at the various stages. The order in which the functions are listed is not intended to indicate a sequence, as many of the functions are interdependent and will overlap in practice.

(1) *Establishment of the client's objectives and priorities*
If the project manager is involved in the conceptual stages of the project, this will be his starting point and should encompass the client's broader organisational objectives as well as the objectives for the envisaged project. This will enable him to provide informed advice upon the alternative construction strategies available and so provide the basis for developing an appropriate brief for the project.

Even if the project manager is not involved until after the client has arrived at his own conclusions and has some firm ideas about the brief, the client's broader objectives should be explored with him. This is to make sure that the client's ideas of what the project will provide are sound and are likely to satisfy those objectives.

(2) *Design of the project organisation structure*
The design of the organisation structure of the project should commence by anticipating the decision points in the process and defining the feedback loops and the relationships of the contributors to each other and to the decision points, as described in the last chapter.

(3) *Identification of the way in which the client is integrated into the project*
This will arise from the design of the organisation referred to in (2) above but merits a separate reference. It is important that the project manager persuade the client that he has to design his organisation to mesh with the project team. Having achieved that, the project manager must ensure that the client responds to the need to integrate with the project team. This will take place at a formal level through meetings but the project manager should seek to ensure that discussions, decisions and the need for those decisions are passed through the appropriate channels of the client's organisation. This will require the project manager to adopt a position close to the client's organisation, and is important for the transmission of information to the client and for the project manager to sense and follow up any changes in the environmental context of the client's organisation that may affect the project.

(4) *Advice on the selection and appointment of the contributors to the project and the establishment of their terms of reference*
The client may require to be advised on these matters. It may even be the case in some circumstances that the client will leave this entirely up to the project manager. It is important that the contributors used on the project have the experience and capability for the particular project and that their approach is compatible with that of the project manager. The project manager is more likely to be able to make this judgement than the client unless the latter is very experienced in construction. The actual terms of appointment of the contributors will, of course, be a decision taken by the client but the project manager should be able to acquaint him with the alternative approaches available and advise on that which is most suitable for the particular project.

This area also includes the terms of appointment of the project manager and the extent of his authority. The project manager can hardly advise on whom to appoint as project manager (!), but he will have to negotiate his appointment with the client. Perhaps the most difficult decisions the client will have to make are whom to appoint to manage the project for him and, secondly, how to form an integration with him from within his own organisation. The degree of authority delegated to the project manager will depend upon the extent to which the client wishes to retain power of approval, as discussed previously.

(5) *Translation of the client's objectives into a brief for the project team and its transmission*

This involves establishment of user needs, the budget, cost and investment plans and, where appropriate, disposal strategies and their correlation. It is at this stage that fundamental misinterpretations occur and opportunities for economies are overlooked which then become enshrined with the development of the brief. Construction of the brief requires considerable knowledge of the performance in use of buildings, from the points of view of value, maintenance and user activity, and the widest spectrum of advice should be obtained and the most appropriate techniques of evaluation of alternatives employed.

The project manager should make sure that the brief is clearly transmitted to other members of the project team and that it is understood by them. There is a perpetual danger that it will be misinterpreted and result in contributors pulling in different directions. This makes it particularly necessary that it is unequivocally drafted.

(6) *Preparation of the programme for the project*

Although this can be thought of as being part of the brief, it is identified separately since it is an area much neglected at the present time, particularly during the early phases of the project and the design stage. The programme should represent a realistic co-ordinated plan of the time needed for the project from the start until, and including, commissioning. As for any plan, it must be carefully monitored, controlled and adapted as necessary.

Although a number of useful techniques exist for programming (e.g. networking and bar charts), none of the professions involved in the early stages of projects tends to specialise in this work and it is often left to the project manager to provide this operational skill himself.

(7) *Activation of the framework of relationships established for the contributors*

Having established the relationships necessary for the project when designing the organisation and agreeing the terms of reference of each contributor, the project manager should ensure that the relationships and responsibilities are activated in the manner intended. He therefore has to be close to the activities of the contributors to ensure that they are in fact performing the work allocated to them and are consulting and taking advice as intended. This activity also covers the work and contribution of the client.

(8) *Establishment of an appropriate information and communication structure*

Much of the information produced for projects is uncoordinated and this can lead to inefficiency in information use and communication, and to misunderstanding. The project manager should lay down formal communication channels and determine the way in which information is to be presented. This is a particularly difficult problem as there is still a need for national and international data co-ordination systems to be adopted. Project management firms may devise and develop their own computer-aided data co-ordination system for this purpose and there is evidence of this already having taken place. In the absence of such sophisticated systems, there is still the opportunity to require the project team to produce information in a compatible manner.

Communication channels present a less intractable problem and the project manager should design them to ensure that all relevant parties are kept up to date formally on events on the project. Of special importance in this respect is communication with the client. The responsibility for preparing co-ordinated reports for the client will rest with the project manager, who should agree the need and frequency of such reports with the client when designing the integrating mechanism between the client and the project team.

(9) *Convening and chairing meetings of appropriate contributors at all stages*

This represents the formal aspects of the integration of the contributors alongside which informal integration will be taking place. Such meetings will act as formal checks on the achievement of the brief in terms of design, cost and time. As such they must be action minuted so that control can be exercised against the decisions of previous meetings. Naturally, minutes should be circulated to all contributors.

It is important that the project manager should be conscious of the need for meetings and adjust their frequency to suit the particular stage of development of the project.

(10)   *Monitoring and controlling feasibility studies, design and production to ensure that the brief is being satisfied, including adherence to the budget, investment and programme plans*

This is the 'meat' of the project manager's work and is predominantly concerned with control. He is responsible for taking appropriate action to ensure that the project proceeds to plan. The project manager should be prepared to advise the client if his requirements cannot be met or if an alternative strategy to that contained in the brief emerges as more appropriate to the client's needs.

The project manager will be activating the feedback loops built into the process and measuring progress against the project's objectives, monitoring the project's environment and responding as necessary. The project manager will not therefore be concerned only with the state of the project's development at the time he takes a feedback sample but must also be concerned with forecasting events in the future to anticipate potential problems and attempt to resolve them before they arrive.

Clients generally do not feel that they are well informed about their projects and the responsibility for this lies with the project manager. Thus, as well as involving the client closely in his project, as previously discussed, the project manager should keep the client formally up to date on forecasts of the project team's performance so that action can be taken by the client in advance of a forecast event that may affect his organisation, e.g. delay in completion of the project.

The individual tasks will vary from project to project, but the types of task over which the project manager will have to exercise control and co-ordination are broadly as follows:

Land acquisition
Applications for planning consent
Outline design strategies
Budget and investment strategies

Advice on finance, taxation and grants
Detailed design
Design cost control
Disposal strategies
Proposals for contractual arrangements for construction
Appointment of the contractor
Appointment of subcontractors
Construction
Cost control during construction
Disposal

In integrating and controlling the contributors undertaking tasks such as those indicated above, the project manager should ensure that all appropriate contributors are involved in each task and that the output of the tasks is compatible with the project objectives in terms of design, cost and time. In order to achieve this, the project manager needs to assure himself that the contributors are maintaining an appropriate level of progress in carrying out the tasks and are employing suitable techniques. In addition, he will need to satisfy himself that the contributors are using an appropriate number of staff of the right calibre and experience. For this purpose he will have to develop appropriate relationships with the contributors and they will have to accept his authority to satisfy himself on these issues. If he is dissatisfied, he will require authority to ensure that the contributors respond to any reservation he has in this respect. This represents a sensitive area and although the project manager should be able to achieve his requirements by informal means, he may on occasion have to fall back on an authority given to him by the client.

(11)   *Contribution to primary and key decisions and to making operational decisions*

The project manager will bring forward to the client alternative proposals upon which primary and key decisions, as discussed previously, will be based and will assist the client in coming to the decision that best satisfies his objectives. Alternatively, the process may have brought forward a single recommendation; he will undertake the presentation to the client.

Within the process, operational decisions, as discussed previously, will have to be made as a result of the activities of the contributors and it should be the project manager's responsibility to make such decisions.

(12)   *Recommendation and control of the implementation of a strategy for disposal or management of the completed project, including commissioning the building and advising on arrangements for running and maintaining it when completed*

This includes the sale or letting of the completed project where appropriate or the 'putting into use' of projects that will be occupied by the owner. In the latter case, maintenance manuals should be provided and 'taught' to the client's personnel.

In commissioning the project, the project manager should involve all the contributors appropriate to this activity so that they can explain to the client's personnel how the project and its services are intended to be used.

(13)   *Evaluation of the outcome of the project against its objectives and against interim reports including advice on future strategies*

This represents the final feedback loop and should provide information on the performance of the project team and the client. The distillation of experience on the project should assist the project team and the client to improve their performance on other projects.

This relatively formal statement of the functions of project management subsumes what is probably the most important role, that of integrator of all contributors. If the project manager were unable to fulfil such a role, it is extremely doubtful whether he could satisfactorily carry out the functions suggested.

A list of functions such as this tends to stress the inanimate parts of projects yet one of the most important components is understanding the human aspects of projects, which can only be achieved by working through people. A vitally important part of the project manager's work is therefore concerned with listening and talking to the members of the project team. This will enable him to anticipate problems that lie at the interface of the work of the contributors, and together with them to come up with solutions.

A particularly difficult area in this respect is the relationship with the contractor and subcontractors when the project has been let by competition. The standard forms and conditions of contract often used in such situations tend, because of the formality and financial implications of the conditions, to inhibit informal relationships between the project manager and design team members, and the contractor and subcontractors. Nevertheless, because of the significance of the construction stage to project success, the project manager needs to be able to establish with the contractor the particular problems anticipated in the construction programme and the action necessary to overcome them. This refers in particular to the transmission of information from the designers to the contractors. It could be the case that, by using other methods of appointing the contractor and subcontractors that allow them to be involved in the design stage, these types of problem will, to a large extent, be overcome.

An essential support to the project management functions is the ability of the project manager to understand other people, to identify what makes them tick and hence to be able to motivate them to perform to the limit of their capabilities. The ability to do this arises from the personal characteristics of the project manager.

Finally, and failing all else, the project manager will need to 'arbitrate' in the case of formalised disputes on the project, whether within the design team, with the construction team or between them, in order to safeguard the client's position. The project manager's knowledge that he may at some stage have to adopt such a position will make it more difficult for him to adopt his integrating role, which is of a more conciliatory nature, but the resolution of such conflict is what is expected of project managers.

8 Organisation Structures

INTRODUCTION

The conventional approach to project organisation with the architect as team leader, responsible for both design and management of the project with the contractor appointed on the basis of a competitive tender, still predominates in the U.K. and many other parts of the world. However, in recent years variations on this method have emerged, as well as some rather more innovative approaches to project organisation.

This chapter examines the contribution of alternative approaches to the solution of organisational problems against the features of project organisation previously identified. These features were:

(a) The relationship of project team to the client organisation and the client's influence upon the decision points.
(b) The degree of interdependency of tasks and people generated by the project and the organisation structure.
(c) The degree of differentiation present within the operating system (which ideally should be reduced to a minimum). The level to which it can be reduced will be constrained by the nature of the project.
(d) The level of integration provided by the managing system and the complexity of the managing system itself. Over-elaboration can lead to severe differentiation within the managing system, which should have the capability to match its integrative effort to the degree of differentiation present in the project.

In practice there are three major components to the organisation structure of projects:

(a) The client/project team integrative mechanism.
(b) The organisation of the design team.
(c) The integration of the construction team into the process.

A number of options are available within each of these categories and this results in a large number of possible combinations. The whole range cannot be considered here but the more likely alternatives are analysed. Of course some options within (b) would not be used with some options within (c), e.g. a conventionally organised design team with a design-and-build contract. However, many others are combinable, and have an effect one upon the other, e.g. a conventionally organised design team and management contracting, which could have a profound effect upon how the design team is organised.

CLIENT/PROJECT TEAM INTEGRATION

This aspect has been discussed earlier, and, as was pointed out, the variety of organisation structures of client organisations is vast. It will not be possible for the project team to affect the client's organisation structure other than marginally. It will be up to them to organise themselves to fit in with the client's organisation. It is therefore a case of the project team organising itself so that it has the capability to understand the client's firm and its environment in order that it can respond to the client's requirements and any changes that may be dictated by the client's environment during design and construction.

It will be easier to integrate with some clients than with others. Where the client has in-house expertise in construction, it is to be expected that the dovetailing of the project team with the client will be easier. On the other hand, integration with a client who does not have in-house expertise or, even more difficult, one who has not built previously, will be more of a problem. The response therefore has to come from the project team and the structure of the design and construction teams should be set up so as to reflect the difficulty of integration with the client. For example, if the client is experienced in construction and has in-house expertise, he may appoint a project manager with experience of the construction industry from his own staff. In such a situation, given the right qualities in the project manager, it may well be that a conventionally structured design team under the direction of the project manager would be appropriate and economical. There could well be no case for the appointment of a further project manager from the design team.

Alternatively, the client may be building for the first time and embarking upon a complex project, e.g. the rebuilding of a processing plant. Because of the naivety of the client and the complexity of the project, it may be advisable to appoint a project manager in an executive capacity from outside the client's organisation.

Similarly, as referred to previously, the authority of the project manager will vary depending upon the attitude of the client to delegation. The extent of delegation of authority is likely to be strongly influenced by whether the project manager is 'in-house' to the client's organisation or external to it. There will be a tendency for clients to delegate more to an 'in-house' project manager and such a project manager will also have greater access to the internal workings of the client organisation. Even in such a case delegation may not be high if the client's organisation is hierarchical and bureaucratic.

There can be no hard and fast rules for the integration of the client and the project team. The mechanism that is selected should be the result of an analysis of the client's organisational structure, his needs and the complexity of the project. The objective of such a mechanism should be simplicity within the constraints of the need to identify clearly decision points and the client's involvement with the decision-making process.

DESIGN TEAM ORGANISATION

CONVENTIONAL STRUCTURE

The conventional structure of architect responsible for design and management with other consultants acting for the architect and with estate management functions being directly responsible to the client is illustrated diagrammatically in fig. 8.1. In such an arrangement the contractor is normally appointed after the design is substantially complete, usually by competition, although he may be appointed on the basis of a negotiated tender or by some other means.

In many cases each contributor will be from an independent professional practice, the contractor also being independent of the other contributors, yet the contributors will be interdependent in terms of the project. The more complex the client organisation and/or the project, the more interdependent will be the tasks to be carried out in achieving the project and the more the contributors will rely upon each other to carry out their work satisfactorily.

Such a structure produces a high level of differentiation between the contributors, which demands a high level of integration. The problem of providing the appropriate level of integration is compounded by

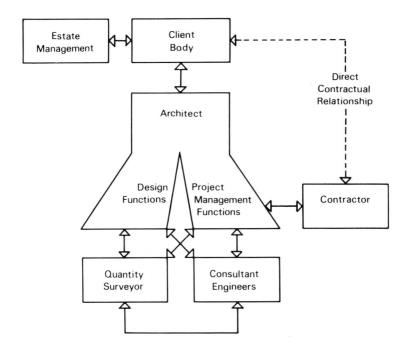

Fig. 8.1 Conventional structure.

the fact that the managing system is not differentiated from the operating system. That is, the architect is attempting to fulfil dual roles. One is in the operating system - design - the other in the management of the project. There is therefore a high potential for someone in this position not to be able to exercise objectivity in decision-making. In addition, whoever is in this position is placed under severe pressure by being required to undertake tasks that frequently require what are often incompatible skills - design and management. This does not mean that adequate project management cannot in any circumstances take place in such a structure, only that it may be extremely difficult to achieve and will require a person of exceptional talent to be able to fulfil both roles satisfactorily in the complex environment within which construction takes place.

Although this does not have to be the case, such a structure has a tendency to restrict access of the other contributors to the client and hence the decision-making process. The perceived personal relationship between the client and his architect, particularly with clients new to construction, can inhibit the client from approaching the other contributors for direct advice. As there is no one solely in a project management role, there is a danger that apposite advice is not taken, which will be to the detriment of the outcome of the project.

Integration within the design team can therefore be difficult to achieve in this structure, as can the integration of the design team with the client. This situation is made even more difficult by appointing the contractor in competition. The direct contract with the client which this produces reinforces the contractor's differentiation from the design team. Similarly, the frequent exclusion from the design team of the estate manager, where he is required, also adds to differentiation.

The situation can arise in which the quantity surveyor, estate manager or engineer is the first contributor to be appointed and subsequently has advised the client on the appointment of the other consultants. In each of these cases the result will tend to be similar to the situations described in fig. 8.1. That is, the first appointed contributor assumes project management responsibilities alongside his professional functions, leading to a potential lack of objectivity in weighing factors from other contributors and to integration problems equally as difficult as those described above.

The degree of differentiation would be reduced if all the design team contributors were from the same interdisciplinary practice but, even within such a practice, if its members are organised on conventional lines with the team leader exercising both professional and project management functions, the main hindrance to objectivity and integration would still remain. However, such a practice has a better opportunity of overcoming problems created by differentiation and of generating sound integration for individual projects than if projects are designed using independent practices. A parallel situation would exist if all the design contributors were in house to the client's organisation (e.g. a government department, a local authority or a large industrial concern). A major additional advantage in this situation would be the potentially high level of integration with the client, as client and design team would be under the same organisational umbrella.

Taking this argument a stage further, the organisation that should, theoretically, have the least differentiation and the greatest opportunity to achieve full client integration is one that has a construction capacity as well as a design capability within the client organisation, for example a local authority direct labour organisation or a contractor/developer. However, each of these examples can present different types of problem, for example control and motivation in the case of the direct labour department, and definition and conflict of objectives for the contractor/developer.

NON-EXECUTIVE PROJECT MANAGEMENT[1]

A structure often employed by interdisciplinary practices, either private practices or in house to the client's organisation, is one that includes a non-executive project manager, sometimes called a co-ordinator, who operates in parallel with the other contributors, as illustrated in fig. 8.2. The role undertaken by the person in this position is based upon communication and co-ordination activities and is not concerned with decision-making. In these circumstances responsibility for the success or failure of the project will be with the firm or the particular in-house department and not with the non-executive project manager within the team as would be the case with a project manager acting in an executive capacity. There is therefore less pressure for the project manager or the firm to define the project manager's role and authority. What pressures there are will be internal to the firm or departments, depending upon how they see the role of the project manager within the team.

Such a role is unlikely to have a significant effect upon the quality of integration of the design team with the client's organisation but could, if exercised with skill and received positively by members of the design team, assist in integrating the design team. If exercised unskilfully or in an uncooperative climate, it could emphasise differentiation within the team without contributing to integration. The authority of the non-executive project manager is likely to be weak and hence his ability to contribute will be determined by the commitment of the firm and the attitude of the individual members of the design team to his role.

A non-executive project manager could be used where the contributors are from separate practices. Such a role is likely to be undertaken by one of the independent firms contributing to the design, although it is conceivable that it could be undertaken by a firm solely devoted to project management. The result is unlikely to contribute much to the project management process, although any improvement in co-ordination and communication would be

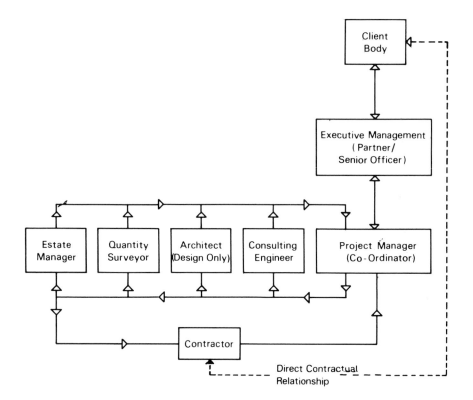

Fig. 8.2   Non-executive project management structure.

of benefit. The lack of an executive function would mean that project management would be split between the non-executive role and the decision-making role, which would still be undertaken by the architect, partner or senior officer. The potential benefit of improved co-ordination and communication may well be more than offset by the complexity of the management system which emerged. The major management role will still not be separated from the operating system and, in fact, if the non-executive role were shared with an operating role, this situation would be further compounded.

EXECUTIVE PROJECT MANAGEMENT[1]
An executive project management role is undertaken by a firm or person independent of the other contributors to the process, as illustrated in fig. 8.3. Similarly, if the design team is part of an

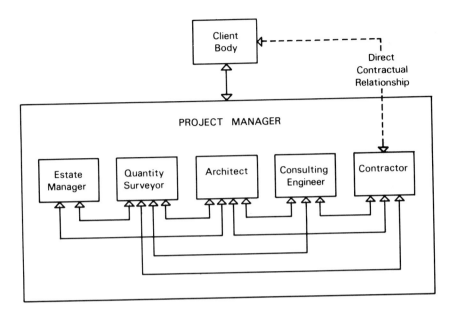

Fig. 8.3   Executive project management structure.

interdisciplinary practice or in house to the client, it will be undertaken by a member who is also independent of the other contributors. In such a structure the project management activity occupies a dominant role in relation to the other contributors, and although they operate as a team, the project manager will make the decisions that are within the purview of the contributors. He will tend to be the sole *formal* point of reference to the client for the purpose of agreeing and transmitting the decisions that must be made by the client. In addition, the project manager will be concerned with controlling, monitoring and maintaining the project team, as discussed previously. These activities are far more dynamic and purposeful than the co-ordination and communication activities of the non-executive project manager and do, of course, subsume them.

It is necessary that the firm or person undertaking this role ensures that responsibility and authority are clearly established with both the client and the other contributors to the project. Although this is difficult to achieve, the benefits of producing a situation in which the roles of the contributors are clearly established are significant. It is, of course, unrealistic for the project manager to accept responsibility for the technical work of the specialist contributors, but responsibility for progress and for budgeting control are possible given the authority to report back to the client if contributors are not performing satisfactorily. However, in practice, the project manager should work in a collaborative manner with the contributors and his major role would be one of facilitating the work of all the contributors so that the project is developed by a team approach. His primary concern would be that appropriate decisions are taken by both the client and the project team at the right time.

In an interdisciplinary practice or in house to the client, the responsibility for the project is clearly with the firm or the department, respectively. The authority of the project manager will be decided internally in the case of an interdisciplinary practice and it is unlikely that the client would exert as great an influence as he would over an in-house department.

The major benefit claimed for the executive project management structure is that management becomes clearly separated from the operating system. That is, no person is charged with carrying out both design activities, be they architecture, engineering or quantity surveying, and project management activities. This allows concentration upon the management needs of the project and makes it possible for conflicting professional advice to be considered more objectively so that decisions which are in the best interests of the project as a whole can be made or recommended.

The structure facilitates integration with the client because the person responsible for managing the project within the client's organisation can readily identify the management responsibility within the design team and is likely to have empathy with the person in this position. This should facilitate the decision-making process, particularly within the client's organisation. A major role of the project manager would be the planning and programming of the project, which would include identifying the contributors and their roles. In doing this he should recognise the differentiation generated by the particular project. He should be in a position to judge the integrative demands and should design mechanisms to cope with them. It is to be expected, therefore, that he will be intimately involved with the client in determining how the organisation for the project should be structured and in deciding the firms and people who will undertake the various roles.

In certain circumstances the client's organisation has personnel who can undertake the executive project manager's role without the need to appoint someone from outside the client's organisation. This arrangement can contribute significantly to the ease of integration between the client and the design team, provided, of course, that the project manager has sufficient status within the client's organisation and can command the respect of the design team. If not, there may be a tendency for the design team to bypass the project manager and seek higher authority in the client's organisation. In this case the role of the project manager would be seriously undermined with resultant confusion in the decision-making process. A similar situation can arise when the project manager is outside the client's organisation, and the solution will be in the attitude which the client takes to resolving the situation.

The person appointed from within the client's organisation to liaise with the design team when an executive project manager has been appointed from an outside organisation is also often called a project manager and it is therefore important to recognise their different roles.

It is also important to recognise that if a person in the design team who is a member of one of the firms contributing in a professional capacity (e.g. quantity surveyor, engineer) is given the title of project manager and ascribed specific responsibilities and authority in this capacity, this does not constitute an executive project management structure as described here. It is in fact a variation on the conventional structure as he will be acting in the same way as the architect traditionally acts, and some of the objectivity of the executive structure would be lost.

INTEGRATION OF THE CONSTRUCTION TEAM

The degree to which the construction team can be integrated into the process at the design stage is determined by the tendering arrangements which are made for obtaining the price for construction. This is obviously a key decision as it has a fundamental effect upon the organisation of the whole process. The most common method is by a lump sum competitive tender after the design has been substantially completed. A number of other methods are now available, but not yet commonly used, which provide for more constructive integration of the contractor.

Competitive lump sum tendering after completion of the design provides the least opportunity for integration as this method requires that the contractor who is to construct the project cannot be involved in the design stage. In addition, during construction it is often difficult to integrate the design team with the construction team as the split between design and construction appears, in many cases, to create a psychological barrier between the two groups. The contractor will often feel that the design has been carried out by people who do not understand construction methods and who seem to him to be providing the wrong drawings at the wrong time. The designers may adopt the view that the contractor is only concerned with profit and not with providing the service that will provide the project they require. Whether such views are correctly held or not does not overcome the fact that on conventionally organised projects, the greatest degree of differentiation occurs between the designers, normally represented by the architect, and the contractor.

If the project is managed by an executive project manager, his greatest integrative effort is likely to be centred around this interface. If the project is organised conventionally, problems of integration at this point will be extremely difficult to resolve if the architect is both designer and project manager and has to integrate himself with the contractor. The difficulties of integrating this interface are compounded still further by the use of subcontractors, both nominated and domestic. Subcontractors nominated by the architect will have a strong allegiance to the architect while having to work in a contractual arrangement and under the direction of the contractor. Domestic subcontractors hired directly by the contractor will tend to hold the same views as the contractor towards the designers.

Many of the recently developed methods of appointing contractors have been aimed at allowing them to be better integrated into the design team while still allowing an element of competition in obtaining a price for the project.

TWO-STAGE TENDERING

In order to maintain competition in a similar form to the conventional method, yet allow the contractor to be involved to some degree in the design stage, two-stage tendering emerged in the late 1960s. In the first stage, selected contractors are invited to tender. Their tenders are based on a notional bill of quantities in which the items are fully described and the quantities are hypothetical but of the order of the magnitude anticipated in the proposed project.

The successful tenderer is then involved in the further development of the design as a member of the team.

A bill of quantities is prepared for the fully developed scheme and is priced by the successful tenderer using the rates, where applicable, in the first-stage tender and negotiating other rates on the basis of the original tender. The result of this process is the price for the project.

This approach assists in the integration of the contractor into at least part of the design process but does not fully exploit the potential benefit to the project of involving the contractor from the beginning. Perhaps one of the greatest benefits is the opportunity to involve the contractor in selection of the specialist subcontractors.

Designers are often sceptical about the contribution a contractor may make to the design of a project but this is one of the aspects the project manager must overcome in integrating the contractor into the design stage. The advice the contractor can give regarding the constructional implications of design decisions and construction methods and processes is likely to be recognised by the designers only after the event. This makes the project manager's task that much more difficult. It also illustrates the fact that integration of the contractor into the design process is less likely to happen in the conventional process where the decision to integrate would have to be made by designers.

Two-stage tendering represents a 'trade-off' between integration of the contractor into the design stage against a conventional approach to competition. It is one of the earlier approaches to integration of the contractor.

SERIAL TENDERING

Serial tendering is used to obtain tenders for a number of similar projects. Contractors bid on the basis of a notional bill of quantities and normally the lowest is accepted. The prices in the notional bill are used for a series of projects, the number, timing and size of which are indicated to the tenderers before bidding.

The actual price for each separate contract is calculated by using the rates submitted in the notional bill. On the face of it, this procedure allows the contractor to be integrated from the beginning of the design of each building in the series for which he has been successful. However, this is rather artificial as the majority of the design decisions will have been made before production of the notional bill so that although the contractor may be integrated, his effective influence on the design stage is limited. Nevertheless, there is a distinct advantage over the conventional approach as it allows discussion with the contractor about such things as subcontractors, plant, programming, etc. during the design of each project in the series.

NEGOTIATED TENDERS

The use of negotiated tenders does not rely upon a competitive element in selecting the contractor. The contractor is selected on the basis of reputation and will probably have worked satisfactorily for the client and/or design team previously. The price for construction will be agreed with the contractor following negotiation between the quantity surveyor and the contractor. There are a number of variations in the approach adopted, often including some type of target cost. Whichever approach is used, the effect on the organisation structure for the project will be similar. Under this arrangement the contractor can be involved in the design process at whatever point the client or project manager decides.

Integration of the contractor can achieve the highest possible level using this approach, but on many negotiated contracts the contractor is still not brought into the process until the design is well advanced and one of the major advantages of this approach is lost.

Naturally, such an arrangement requires a high level of trust between the client, design team and construction team. It is often said that a negotiated price will be higher than a competitive one so the integration of the contractor may be traded off against a higher price. However, the benefits to be gained from integration - earlier start on site and earlier completion, constructionally sound designs, cost-saving advice from the contractor, etc. - may more than counterbalance the lack of competition. Within this framework, subcontracts may be negotiated or competitive, giving a facility for closer integration of subcontractors if their use is considered beneficial.

MANAGEMENT CONTRACTING

This approach is basically different from those previously described, as it is a method of integrating contracting expertise into the design stage of a project on a fee basis rather than a method of obtaining tenders and letting contracts. The objective is to incorporate the management contractor into the design team on an equivalent basis to all the other consultants. The management contractor would be responsible for the construction work, all of which is carried out by subcontractors who may be appointed in competition or by negotiation.

The project is split into 'packages' for tendering purposes. Design, cost control and construction are integrated into the overall programme. The contractor provides advice on the availability and procurement of materials and components and the 'buildability' of the proposed design. He is involved in the compilation of the cost plan for the project and monitors and provides financial data concerning the project during the construction phase. The management contractor does not carry out the construction work directly but may provide certain central facilities (e.g. canteen, welfare, scaffolding). However, the management contractor sees his role as that of a manager.

It can be seen that management contracting is a positive approach to the integration of construction expertise into the design process. Its main thrust is management of the construction aspects of the project in both the design and construction phases with status equivalent to that of all other professional contributors.

Whereas the subcontractors will be in a strongly differentiated position similar to that of the contractor in the conventional process, the management contracting activity will be primarily concerned with integrating them. This is rather different from the situation with a conventional structure as the management contractor's objective is that of achieving satisfaction for the client and he does not have the entrepreneurial interest of the contractor employed under a conventional arrangement. This is in fact transferred to the subcontractors but in this case there is an integrating mechanism acting directly for the client.

The person responsible for project management will have the task of integrating the management contracting activity into the design team. If this is the architect, then it may be difficult, although it should not be so if the architect instigated the use of management contracting in the first instance. However, frequently it is the client who decides that management contracting should be used. In this case it is important that the remainder of the team is structured in a compatible manner. The allegiances and attitudes at large in the construction industry may make extremely difficult the integration of management contracting into a design team whose other members are unsympathetic to the idea. This may mean that either a strong client or a project manager with sound authority is necessary to gain greatest benefit from this approach.

SEPARATE TRADES CONTRACTING

Separate trades contracting is used as a generic title for approaches that can be seen to be similar to the idea of management contracting. In each case there is no main contractor appointed for the project but instead fee-earning members of the project team organise subcontractors to undertake the work. The idea is not new: Scotland was the last region of the U.K. that used it as the normal method of arranging the construction stage, and it is still regularly used in other parts of the world.

In its most recent form in the U.K. it is referred to as *alternative methods of management* (A.M.M.)[2]. Although there is no main contractor, there may be a need for a general builder to work alongside specialist contractors and to provide some central services. However, the site architect/manager is responsible for running the site. He directs the activities of subcontractors either through their supervisor or directly to the men on site. The subcontractors are appointed by competition or negotiation for packages of work. In effect the site architect/manager replaces the main contractor's site agent and provides the site with direct and constant design supervision. He is often supported by a quantity surveyor who arranges the contracts and he must have ready access to the client whose involvement on site is higher than on conventional projects. It is claimed that the main advantages are that communication is as direct as possible from client to architect to tradesmen, that the human element is all important and the client's interest is best served by people committed primarily to his project rather than their profession or trade.

Compared with management contracting, A.M.M. does not incorporate construction expertise as such in the design stage but relies upon the ability of the architect in this respect. Given an architect with the appropriate background, this would be satisfactory. If the architect's knowledge of construction problems is not so great, his proximity to the tradesmen and his presence continually on site where many of the drawings are prepared could overcome deficiencies provided he was prepared to take advice.

The A.M.M. technique produces a different approach to the problem from that of management contracting. It aims to reduce differentiation between people working on the project with the result that less integration is required to produce a simpler management and operating system structure. Nevertheless, the architect has to operate in a designer/manager role, which could lead to conflict of objectives, and further development may see the site architect/manager taking a more management-orientated role.

The location of the architect on site eliminates the territory determinant of differentiation and will improve the effectiveness of the management process. Whereas management contracting puts in more management to solve the problem, A.M.M. aims to reduce the need for integrative effort.

Other separate trades contracting approaches are 'cost plus contracts' of various types. They are basically similar to the above, except that subcontractors are reimbursed their actual expenditure, plus profit, often only within set total cost targets. The management implications are similar to those outlined above and demand similar levels of involvement of designers in managing the construction stage. They have not received the detailed attention in recent years that management contracting and A.M.M. have, as they are really contractual arrangements and not approaches to management. They are rarely used except for emergency works as they can be expensive. They can, of course, also be used for general contracting as well as for separate trades contracting.

DESIGN-AND-BUILD

Design-and-build contracts, also commonly known as package deals or turnkey contracts, are arrangements that do not separate design and construction between firms. One firm offers the total package of design and construction. The opportunity to provide effective integration of the process is therefore theoretically higher in this approach than in more conventional methods. However, in the U.K. the large majority of firms offering this type of service originated as building contractors and many also offer competitive contracting as well as a design-and-build service. There is therefore a tendency for firms to be orientated towards construction activity, which may have detrimental consequences for the integration of design and a subsequent effect upon its quality. The relationships that emerge

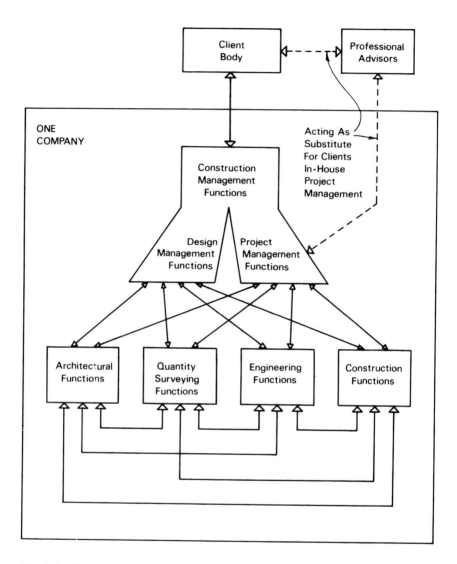

Fig. 8.4   Design-and-build structure (construction dominant).

may be as shown in fig. 8.4. For such a structure the client would need to be assured that the construction management emphasis is not allowed to dominate the project management needs of the project. A structure which is more likely to be acceptable to the client is shown in fig. 8.5, in which it can be seen that project management is allowed to dominate, and design and construction management are integrated in an equivalent relationship.

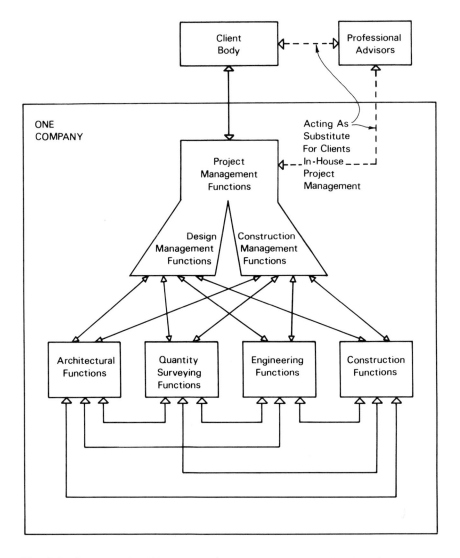

Fig. 8.5   Design-and-build structure (project management dominant).

This latter arrangement is only likely to be adopted by a construction firm which has an 'in-house' design capability that is sufficient for the project. If the firm has to 'subcontract' design, then the relationships that emerge are likely to be similar to a conventional arrangement in terms of the difficulty of integration. However, the client will still retain the advantage of having only one company responsible contractually to him for the whole project.

Similarly, the responsibility for subcontractors for specialist construction will be totally with the design-and-build firm and integration will not normally be complicated by nominated subcontractor relationships.

This approach may potentially provide the most effective integration but there remains difficulty in integrating the project team and the client. The client needs to protect his position so that the project he receives on completion fulfils his requirements. He should have a clear conception of his objectives, but those of the design-and-build firm may at times conflict with those of the client.

If, for instance, a problem needs resolving, in which the achievement of the best design solution conflicts with the method of construction, the design-and-build firm may seek to solve the problem by opting for ease of construction at the expense of the best design solution. Other similar problems may occur, for instance economy versus form of construction, speed versus construction method, etc. The client will be in a position to resolve situations to his benefit if he has sufficient in-house expertise to understand the issues and the appropriate contract conditions that allow him to act to produce a result to his benefit. If he has not, then he will need professional advice upon which to act.

Professional advisers in this capacity would act as a substitute for the client's in-house project management team as shown on figs. 8.4 and 8.5. Integration between the professional advisers and the management structure of the design-and-build firm would have to be carefully designed to ensure that it had effective lines of communication and authority, which would have to be made explicit in the contract conditions e.g. whether they are in an advisory or executive position. Naturally, this implies that the professional advisers should be closely involved in drafting the conditions of contract and in establishing the project.

An extension of the design-and-build approach that has gained more acceptance in recent years in the U.K. and is more widely used abroad is that, rather than arranging a contract with one selected contractor, competition takes place for both design and price. Alternatively, an upper limit on the price may be fixed so that essentially competition is based primarily on design. The management arrangements with the successful bidder would be identical to those discussed earlier for one selected firm but either the client's in-house team or his professional advisers would need to evaluate the submissions against the client's criteria to advise on the bid to be accepted. In such an arrangement, bidders would be provided with details of the client's requirements, which would normally include a performance specification. These details would form the basis of the criteria against which bids would be judged. Therefore integration of the professional advisers with the client or integration within the client's organisation with its own in-house team is of paramount importance in drafting the client's requirements for the bidders and in evaluating the bids.

ORGANISATION MATRIX

At their simplest level, organisation structures of projects can be seen to consist of three major components - the client, the design team and the contractor. The client's experience of construction, the organisation of the design team and the method of appointment of the contractor will have a fundamental influence on the effectiveness of the project organisation. Examples of the range are:

(a) Client

    (i)   No construction expertise, a senior manager liaises between client and project team.

    (ii)   In-house expertise available, project manager appointed within client organisation.

(b) Design team

    (i)   Conventional organisation.

    (ii)   Non-executive project manager.

    (iii)   Executive project manager.

(c) Contractor's appointment

    (i)   Selective competitive tender.

    (ii)   Two-stage competitive tender.

    (iii)   Competitive serial tender.

    (iv)   Negotiated tender.

    (v)   Management contract.

    (vi)   Separate trade contracts.

    (vii)   Design-and-build (overlaps with (b) above).

There are a number of variations within these classes, but they represent the more common classifications and themselves produce a 2 X 3 X 7 matrix, giving forty-two alternative arrangements.

Each arrangement will present certain advantages and disadvantages and should be selected for use in circumstances that suit the particular project. The features of each arrangement are as summarised briefly in table 8.1.

Table 8.1   Matrix of project organisation structures

	Matrix	
Client	Design team	Contractor's appointment
(1) No construction expertise	Conventional	Selective competition

Comments
This is the traditional arrangement and relies upon the architect as designer and manager, with the client having a limited management contribution to his project. The contractor is not integrated into the design phase. Suitable for relatively simple projects in terms of both complexity of construction and environment for which client's requirements are clear

(2) No construction expertise	Conventional	Two-stage, competitive

Comments
Opportunity to use contractor's expertise during part of design phase depending upon when first-stage tenders are initiated. Gives opportunity to speed up programme by overlapping construction and some design work. Appears to be a half-hearted attempt to integrate the contractor

(3) No construction expertise	Conventional	Competitive serial

Comments
As (2) above but used where a number of similar buildings are required for the same client

Table 8.1 (continued)

	Matrix	
Client	Design team	Contractor's appointment
(4) No construction expertise	Conventional	Negotiated

Comments
This arrangement enables the contractor to be integrated at a very early stage in the project. Relies upon the architect as designer/manager being prepared to use and trust the contractor's expertise. Suitable for complex projects and/or environments

(5) No construction expertise	Conventional	Management contractor

Comments
In management terms, similar to (4) above but allows for competition for construction work. Still relies upon the architect as designer/manager being prepared to use and trust the contractor's expertise. The management contractor is acting as another consultant with responsibility for arranging and organising subcontractors and may be more acceptable to other members of the design team in this capacity. Potential conflicts between architect acting in a management capacity as well as being designer and the management role of the management contractor. Suitable for complex projects and/or environments. Illustrated in fig. 8.6

(6) No construction expertise	Conventional	Separate trade contracts

Comments
Potentially high in integration by direct contact between the design team, particularly the architect and subcontractors on site which could be extended into the design phase. Reduces differentiation of major management components by eliminating a separate general contractor function. Requires an architect leader who is strongly management orientated and objective about the often conflicting demands of design and construction. Illustrated in fig. 8.7

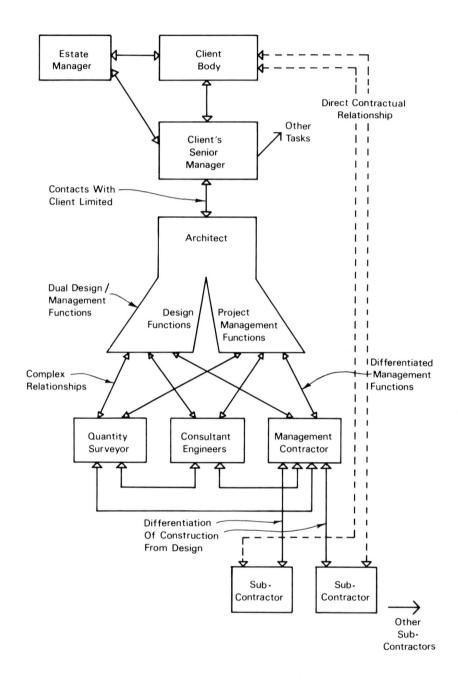

Fig. 8.6   Diagram of type 5 structure.

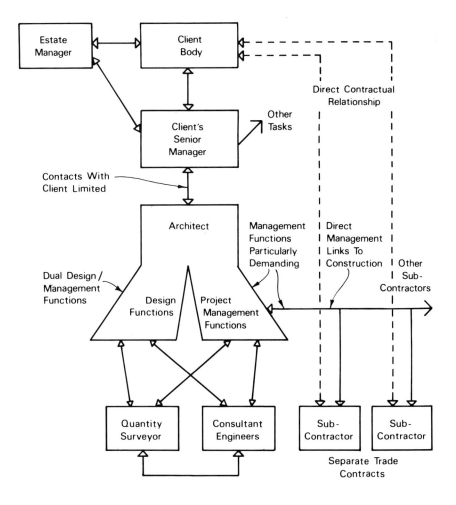

Fig. 8.7 Diagram of type 6 structure.

Table 8.1 (continued)

Matrix		
Client	Design team	Contractor's appointment
(7) No construction expertise	Conventional	Design-and-build

Comments

This arrangement would not be used as described. The conventional design team would act as consultants to the client to monitor the design-and-build contract. As the client has no in-house expertise, some professional advice would be required to act as the client's representatives in dealing with the design-and-build contractor. The conventional design team in this context would probably consist of one or two professional advisers (or a firm). Integration should be strong within the design-and-build firm but the potential weakness is in the integration with the client when he has no in-house expertise, even though he has appointed advisers. Illustrated in figs 8.4 and 8.5

(8) In-house expertise	Conventional	Selective competition
(9) In-house expertise	Conventional	Two-stage competition
(10) In-house expertise	Conventional	Competitive serial
(11) In-house expertise	Conventional	Negotiated
(12) In-house expertise	Conventional	Management contractor
(13) In-house expertise	Conventional	Separate trade contracts
(14) In-house expertise	Conventional	Design-and-build

Comments

This group is similar to (1) to (7) above except that the client has in-house building expertise available and appoints a project manager from within his own organisation.

The result in each case is that integration between the project team and the client should be closer, provided that the client's own internal integration is effective. A member of the client's organisation appointed project manager should have more time to devote to the project than if a senior manager were doing this job in addition to his normal work. The demands on the architect to exercise his management role effectively are likely to be greater as a result of the pressure exerted by the project manager.

Approaches to appointing the contractor and integrating him into the team other than by selective competitive tender are more likely to be adopted because of the influence of the client's in-house project manager.

Table 8.1 (continued)

Matrix		
Client	Design team	Contractor's appointment

Alternative (14) is unlikely to be used as the in-house project manager should normally have the expertise and capability to monitor the design-and-build contract. Alternative (13) is illustrated as an example in fig. 8.8

(15) No construction expertise	Non-executive project manager	Selective competition
(16) No construction expertise	Non-executive project manager	Two-stage competition
(17) No construction expertise	Non-executive project manager	Competitive serial
(18) No construction expertise	Non-executive project manager	Negotiated
(19) No construction expertise	Non-executive project manager	Management contractor
(20) No construction expertise	Non-executive project manager	Separate trade contracts
(21) No construction expertise	Non-executive project manager	Design-and-build
(22) In-house expertise	Non-executive project manager	Selective competition
(23) In-house expertise	Non-executive project manager	Two-stage competition
(24) In-house expertise	Non-executive project manager	Competitive serial
(25) In-house expertise	Non-executive project manager	Negotiated
(26) In-house expertise	Non-executive project manager	Management contractor
(27) In-house expertise	Non-executive project manager	Separate trade contracts
(28) In-house expertise	Non-executive project manager	Design-and-build

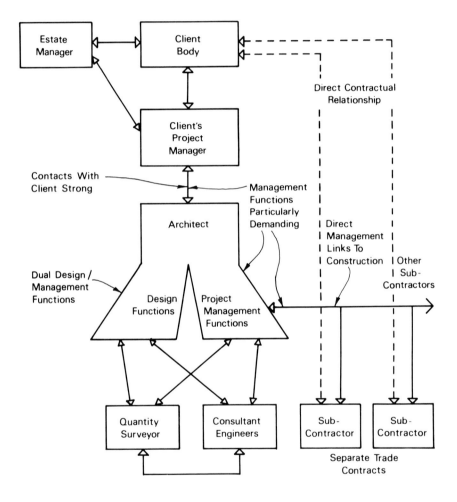

Fig. 8.8 Diagram of type 13 structure.

Table 8.1 (continued)

Matrix		
Client	Design team	Contractor's appointment

Comments

This group corresponds with (1) to (14) above, except that a non-executive project manager is appointed within the project team. As discussed earlier, someone in this position will fill a co-ordination and communication role without authority for executive functions. Provided that the role is recognised and accepted by the other team members, the administration of the project should benefit. But as the decision-making structure and authority pattern remain unaltered, the effect on the management of the project is unlikely to be significant and the comments given for (1) to (14) will apply. The non-executive project manager is likely to be dominated by the designer and in the cases where the client appoints an in-house project manager, he will be particularly easily overridden. Alternative (25) is illustrated in fig. 8.9

(29) No construction expertise	Executive project manager	Selective competition

Comments

Management and design responsibilities are split, which should allow the project manager to concentrate upon management of the project both within and between the design and construction teams and with the client. Probably the most effective way of improving the management of what is still really a conventional structure, suitable for complex projects and/or environments, where it is necessary for the contract to be awarded competitively

(30) No construction expertise	Executive project manager	Two-stage competition

Comments

Comments as for (2). Opportunity is presented for the project manager to ensure that the contractor is properly integrated and makes a contribution to the design phase. It will be up to the project manager to time the first phase so that the contractor's contribution is maximised. Illustrated in fig. 8.10

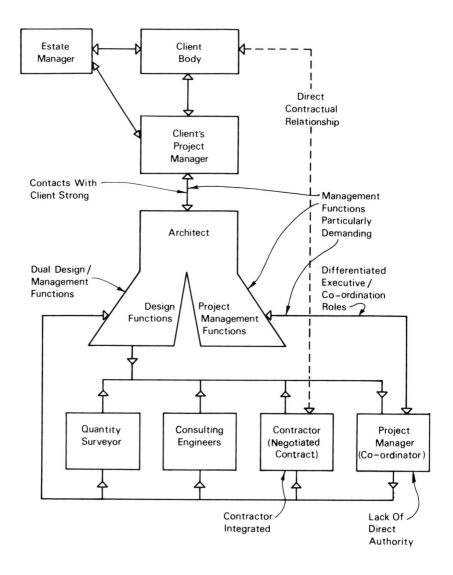

Fig. 8.9   Diagram of type 25 structure.

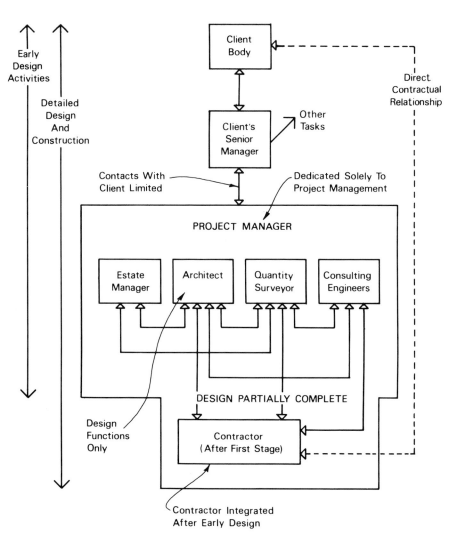

Early
Design
Activities

Detailed
Design
And
Construction

Client
Body

Direct
Contractual
Relationship

Client's
Senior
Manager

Other
Tasks

Contacts With
Client Limited

Dedicated Solely To
Project Management

PROJECT MANAGER

Estate
Manager

Architect

Quantity
Surveyor

Consulting
Engineers

DESIGN PARTIALLY COMPLETE

Design
Functions
Only

Contractor
(After First Stage)

Contractor Integrated
After Early Design

Fig. 8.10   Diagram of type 30 structure.

Table 8.1 (continued)

	Matrix	
Client	Design team	Contractor's appointment
(31) No construction expertise	Executive project manager	Competitive serial

Comments
As (30) above, but where a number of buildings are required for the same client.

(32) No construction expertise	Executive project manager	Negotiated

Comments
This arrangement allows the project manager to establish a tightly integrated team from the very early stages of the project. Allows the project manager to appraise the contribution from all members of the project team objectively. Suitable for very complex projects and/or environments

(33) No construction expertise	Executive project manager	Management contractor

Comments
In management terms similar to (32) above, but allows for competition for construction work. As the management contractor is acting as another consultant, the project manager may be able to integrate him with less constraint than may be the case with (32). Suitable for very complex projects and/or environments. Illustrated in fig. 8.11

(34) No construction expertise	Executive project manager	Separate trade contracts

Comments
Potentially high in integration by direct contact between the design team, particularly the project manager and the subcontractors. Reduces differentiation of major management components by eliminating a separate general or management contractor function. The use of a project manager who is strongly management orientated and objective about the often conflicting demands of design and construction should provide the foundations for a successful project. Suitable for complex projects and/or environments.

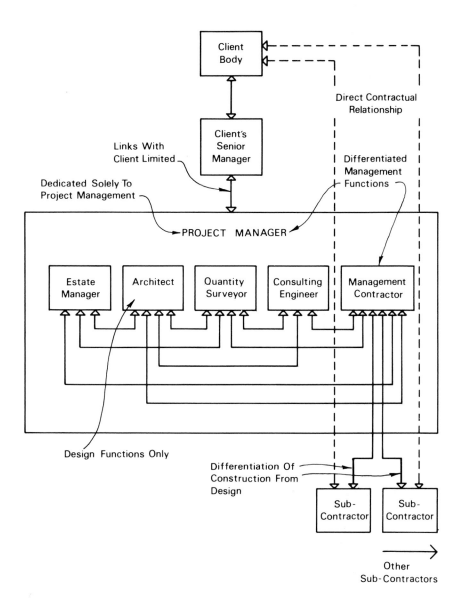

Fig. 8.11 Diagram of type 33 structure.

Table 8.1 (continued)

	Matrix	
Client	Design team	Contractor's appointment
(35) No construction expertise	Executive project manager	Design-and-build

Comments

In this arrangement the executive project manager would not have a supporting design team but would act as the client's representative in monitoring and controlling the design-and-build contract. Integration should be strong within the design-and-build firm. Integration between the client and project manager and between the project manager and the design-and-build firm would depend to a large extent on the relationships established in the formal contract. The project manager should be involved in establishing the contract in which his authority should be clearly established

(36) In-house expertise	Executive project manager	Selective competition
(37) In-house expertise	Executive project manager	Two-stage competition
(38) In-house expertise	Executive project manager	Competitive serial
(39) In-house expertise	Executive project manager	Negotiated
(40) In-house expertise	Executive project manager	Management contractor
(41) In-house expertise	Executive project manager	Separate trade contracts
(42) In-house expertise	Executive project manager	Design-and-build

Comments

This group is similar to (28) to (35) above, except that the client has in-house building expertise available and appoints a project manager from within his own organisation in addition to the executive project manager of the project team. The result in each case is that integration between the project team and the client should be closer, provided that the client's own internal integration is effective.

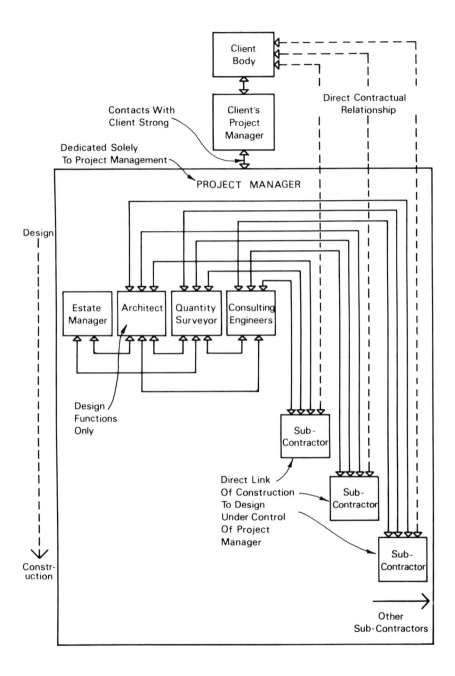

Fig. 8.12   Diagram of type 41 structure.

Table 8.1 (continued)

	Matrix	
Client	Design team	Contractor's appointment

A member of the client's organisation appointed project manager should have more time to devote to the project than a senior manager who may also have to do his routine work. The use of the two project managers should strengthen the integration with the client to the extent that this group of arrangements should represent potentially the strongest management-dominated organisational structure. Alternative (41) is illustrated in fig. 8.12. In particular the use of structures that allow the contractor to be integrated into the team (39, 40, 41) has the potential for full integration and allegiance to objectives of even the most complex projects, the facility for implementing the most rigorous control mechanisms and the opportunity to take the most appropriate advice before decisions are taken.

One of the key issues in the choice of organisation structure lies in the trade-off between the apparent competitiveness of the bid price for the construction work and the early involvement of the contractor in the project team. Although competition for a construction contract may appear to provide the client with the lowest price, it is achieved only at the cost of a potentially less integrated project team, as the contractor cannot be brought into the design team sufficiently early to influence the 'buildability' of the design. The effect of this could be a longer construction period and a higher price because of the difficulty of construction of the proposed design. Hence the competitiveness of the bid may be more imagined than real. In the interests of the total economy of the project, a fully integrated team throughout the whole process may be more beneficial to the client's interests. This factor will be most important in selecting the appropriate structure of the major components of the project organisation to suit the particular circumstances of the project and the needs of the client.

References

1. Walker, A. (1976) *Project Management: A Review of the State of the Art.* London: The Institute of Quantity Surveyors (now the Royal Institution of Chartered Surveyors).
2. Thompson, N. (27 Jan. 1978) 'Alternative Methods of Management'. *Building.*

9 Analysis and Design of Project Management Structures

NEED FOR ANALYSIS AND DESIGN

The mainly theoretical scenario developed so far provides the concepts necessary for analysing project organisations and the basis for a structured approach to their design. Such theory is all very well but it needs translating into techniques that are useful in practice and make a positive contribution to improving the effectiveness of the management of projects in the real world. For analysis, such techniques should be capable of mapping what actually happened on projects. When used for design they should be capable of showing clearly what is expected to happen if the project is to be managed effectively. The predominant need is to design structures that allow people to work together effectively, but there is the parallel need to develop structures that enable the use of appropriate project management techniques.

The increasingly explicit recognition of project management in its own right rather than as something subservient to other professional skills has helped to generate a range of techniques and tools for project control, e.g. critical path networks, line of balance, etc. There is, however, often a gulf between the availability of techniques and their actual use on projects. The opportunity and the will to employ such techniques depend upon a receptive management structure and the effective organisation of contributors. A management structure led by people whose priority is management should result in more widespread use of project control techniques and ensure that contributors to the project are organised to maximise the benefits of such techniques.

It is the responsibility of those exercising project management skills on behalf of clients to design organisation structures appropriate to particular projects and their environments so that the right skills and techniques are used at the right time. This is particularly difficult to achieve in construction as the structures normally used are predominantly conventional and reflect the juxtaposition of traditional professional roles. This tends to inhibit innovation, with the result that the industry and professions are slow to apply new ideas and techniques.

CRITERIA

Techniques for analysing and designing organisational structures should make clear the following aspects of the way in which the project is organised:

(a) the operating system;
(b) the managing system;
(c) the relationship of people in the organisation and their interdependency;
(d) the roles of the people in the organisation;
(e) the position of the decision points and their status, e.g. key, operational;
(f) the contribution of people to each decision and their relationships in arriving at decisions.

An approach that exposes these aspects will give great visibility to the way in which projects are organised. It will show clearly who did what and, perhaps more significantly, who did not. Compared with the traditional pyramidal organisation chart, such an approach would, if used for organisation design, be a dynamic representation of what should happen on a project, or, if used for analysis, what really did happen, rather than being a simplistic, static statement of who is whose boss, without any attempt to relate the people to the project activities and to each other.

TECHNIQUES

Two techniques go some way to satisfying the criteria: *transformed relationships evolved from network data (TREND)* and *linear responsibility charting (LRC)*. In principle, both are based upon a network approach but expose the relationships of the people involved in the project rather than the time relationship of activities, which is the normal use of network techniques.

TREND[1,2] was developed to analyse organisations in a study of temporary management structures. The categories of information required were identified as:

(a) What tasks are to be performed?
(b) Who is responsible for each task?
(c) How do the tasks interrelate?
(d) What is the interaction pattern of the participating departments?
(e) Which tasks and departments are more critical to successful completion?
(f) What is the nature and location of the uncertainties involved?

It was recognised that much of this information could be obtained from a network, but that to answer (e) and (f) a PERT network with three time estimates for activities would be required. The technique was used for examining what the study identified as the two initial variables affecting organisation design: the nature of the tasks and the resource group interdependencies, which were taken as subsuming the above list of questions.

Using TREND it is possible to identify the resource groups responsible for activities contained in the network and the types of interdependencies between resource groups generated by the project. The nature of the tasks was assessed from the level of uncertainty associated with activities, and the critical nature of activities, both of which were represented by the three time estimates of PERT networks.

TREND has the potential to provide a powerful and sophisticated tool for project organisation design where a high level of uncertainty needs to be managed. However, ideally it requires a PERT network with three time estimates or information to this level of detail. In the original study carried out in the U.S.A. it was found that there were very few projects available with this degree of detail in networks. In fact there were only a limited number of projects for which there was a network of any kind. As a corollary the technique has been found to have limited application to long-duration projects with much aggregation of the activities in the project plan. As most construction project plans are of this type, the application and usefulness of TREND may be limited until such time as the construction industry adopts more sophisticated planning techniques.

An alternative approach, which does not require extensive networks to be available and which incorporates within it a technique for building up organisation networks at various levels of detail, has been developed from linear responsibility charting. This first appeared in about 1955[3] but does not appear to have been further developed until about 1975, by Cleland and King.[4] Linear responsibility charting originated as an improvement upon the pyramidal organisation chart so that it shows who participates and to what degree when an activity is performed or a decision made.

LINEAR RESPONSIBILITY ANALYSIS

It was subsequently discovered that LRC could serve as a tool for organisation design and analysis since it can be made to display system interfaces and interrelationships. It was then further advanced into the linear responsibility analysis (LRA) technique in 1980. This method allowed the degree and quality of differentiation, integration and interdependency within an organisation system to be identified and was applied to building projects.[5] Decision points were overlain on the LRA to show the combination of contributors to decisions and their roles.

Although arising from general management thinking, LRA is particularly useful for project management. Its effectiveness lies in its ability to expose both the decision points in the process and the way in which the people in the operating and managing systems are arranged in relation to those decision points. It also allows identification of the activities of the people in the managing and operating systems and of the relationships between them. Thus LRA gives visibility to the arrangement and integration of contributors bringing forward propositions upon which decisions are based. An understanding of how this process works is fundamental to the success of a project organisation and LRA makes a significant contribution.

Starting with the linear responsibility chart (LRC) from which the linear responsibility analysis (LRA) originated, the best way to understand the approach and how information is presented is to examine a typical chart such as that for the design of a building project, shown in fig. 9.1.

The LRC illustrated uses eleven symbols (see page 179 for detailed description) to indicate different types of relationship that may exist between any job position in the organisation structure and any task to be performed. The job positions are listed along the horizontal axis of the matrix and the tasks to be carried out are listed down the vertical axis. In the square where a job position and a task meet, the relationship is indicated by inserting the appropriate symbol. If a job position has no relationship with a task, the square is, of course, left blank.

Legend

- ○ Did The Work
- ▲ Approves
- ▶ Recommends
- ● General Oversight
- ◆ Direct Oversight
- △ Boundary Control
- □ Monitoring
- ◇ Maintenance
- ■ Consultation – Gave Instructions And Information
- ▽ Consultation – Gave Advice And Information
- ⊗ Output Notification Mandatory

MAJOR TASK	Parent Company	Local Board Of Directors	Responsible Director	Project Director	Department Engineer	Managers	Specialist Staff	Workforce	Senior Partner	Project Manager	Manager Structural Engineering	Job Structural Engineer	Manager Services Engineering	Job Services Engineer	Partner Architect	Job Architect	Partner Quantity Surveyor	Job Quantity Surveyor
		Client							Engineers						Architect		Q.S.	
1 Identify Need For Project		●▲	◆▶	△□●		○	▽											
2 Define Outline Requirements		●▲	◆▶	△□◇		○	▽											
3 Establish Budget Estimate		●▲	◆▶	△○					▽									
4 Presentation For Inclusion In 5 Year Plan	▲	●▼	◆	△○					◆▽	▼△◇	△	○	▽		▽		▽	
5 Programme Proposals				▲■●					◆▽	▼△□◇	▽	○	▽		▽	○	○	▽
6 Contractual Proposals				▲■●		▽			▽▶	▼△□◇	◆	○	◆		◆	▽	▽	▽
7 Spatial Proposals				▲■●		▽	▽	▽	◆▽	▼△□◇	◆	▽	▽	○	▽	▽	▽	▽
8 Technical Proposals (Structural)				▲■●		▽	▽	▽	◆▽	▼△□◇	▽	▽	◆	▽	◆	○	▽	▽
9 Technical Proposals (Services)				▲■●		▽	▽	▽	◆▽	▼△□◇	▽	▽	▽	▽	▽	▽	◆	○
10 Technical Proposals (Architectural)				▲■●					◆▽	▼△◇	▽	▽	▽	▽	▽	▽	▽	▽
11 Financial Proposals			▶	▲■●					◆▽									
12 Consolidate Brief	▲	◀▶	▶	▲○													▽	▽
13 Capital Expenditure Presentation				▲▽					●	▼△□◇	◆▽	▽	▽	▽	◆	○	▽	▽
14 Programme Details				▲▽■					●	▼△□◇	◆◆	○	◆	○	▽	▽	▽	▽
15 Working Drawings				▲▽■					●	▼△□◇	▽	▽	▽	◆	▽	▽	▽	▽
16 Technical Details (Structural)				▲▽■					●	▼△□◇	▽	▽	▽	▽	◆	○	▽	▽
17 Technical Details (Services)				▲▽					●	▼△□◇	▽	▽	▽	▽	▽	○	▽	▽
18 Technical Details (Architectural)				▲▽					●	▼△□◇	▽				◆	▽	◆	○
19 Contract Details				■					●	▼△□◇							◆	○
20 Contract Documentation																	◆	○

Fig. 9.1   Typical linear responsibility chart.

For example, for Task 6, 'Contractual Proposals', the partner of the quantity surveying practice prepared the proposals and in doing so consulted the partner of the architectural practice, the managers of the services engineering and structural engineering departments and the senior partner of the engineering practice. He did so under the management of the project manager who was concerned with boundary control, with other activities and with maintenance and monitoring. The project manager finally recommended the proposals to the client's project engineer. The latter approved them as well as being consulted for his instructions and advice during the work and exercising general oversight.

A great benefit of the LRC is the virtue of presenting much in little space in a dynamic form, but it is much more than this. It gives an overall perspective of a project organisation structure which brings to life relationships in a way which more conventional approaches such as pyramidal organisation charts do not. It also gives a basis for further development of more sophisticated and effective techniques of organisation design.

The degree of detail of the tasks selected for the vertical axis is under the control of the designers of the organisation, either as a result of the information which they currently have available or as a result of the particular aspect of organisation design with which they are concerned. Similarly, the job positions can be in the range from individual people to whole departments or firms. The symbols likewise can be selected for the particular purpose. The inherent flexibility of the chart is very valuable to designers in that it allows them to orientate their work to the particular problem they wish to study.

Cleland and King[4] enhanced the LRC by visualising it as an input-output device, as shown in fig. 9.2. The input is the person in the job position with the 'does the work' relationship to the task, and the output is the completion of the task. The inputs-outputs (or 'does the work' relationships) are then transformed into schematic form, as shown in fig. 9.3. The connected boxes containing the job position which 'do the work' and the tasks they carry out form the operating system through which the project is achieved. To this schematic are added the job positions of those who are involved in managing the process together with the symbols representing their specific management functions in connection with each task. These are placed in loops above the task boxes

▲ Approves
◇ Boundary Control
△ Maintenance
□ Monitoring
○ Does The Work
⊗ Output Mandatory
● General Supervision
▽ Consulted

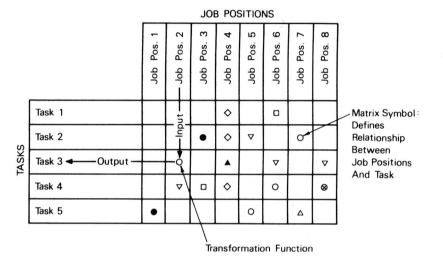

Fig. 9.2   LRC matrix (showing input-output applications).

and are known as the control loops. The control loops represent the managing system of the project. People in relationships other than in the operating or managing systems, mainly in consulting roles, are then added as shown. When completed for the whole project, the schematic LRC shows the way in which the tasks are connected and how people act and interact within the organisation in carrying out the project.

This presentation clarifies the operating system (the linked tasks) through which the project is carried out, and the managing system (the job positions in the control loops) which controls the operating system and the relationships of others who contribute.

A further development of the LRC with the title linear responsibility analysis involves the addition of further systems information to give a sharper view of the system as a whole. This total systems picture of the project enables an objective assessment to be made

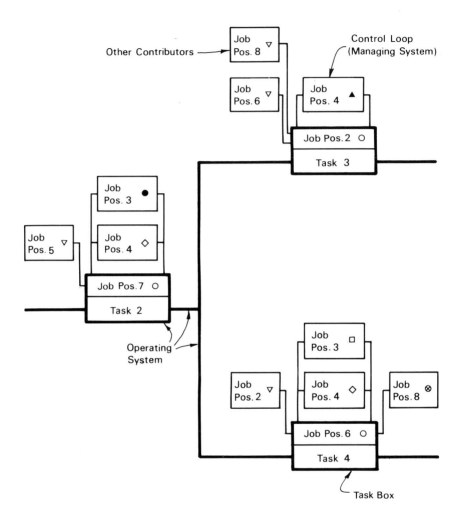

Fig. 9.3   Schematic LRC.

of the level of integration necessary for the system to work effectively. It also enables weaknesses in the system to be identified. If necessary, the system can be redesigned at those points or alternatively particular attention can be paid to integration. This development, as illustrated in fig. 9.4, adds the following to the schematic LRC:

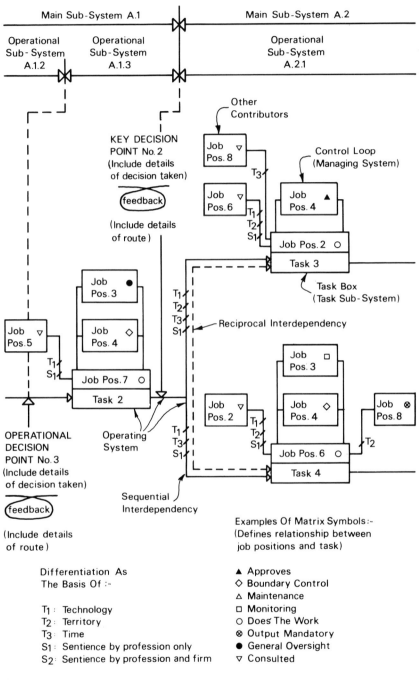

Fig. 9.4   Linear responsibility analysis in principle.

(a) *Interdependency:* The type of interdependency between tasks is shown, sequential interdependency by a solid line and reciprocal by a broken line. The type of interdependency influences the degree and type of integration required. Reciprocal interdependency requires greater integrative effort than sequential and needs a more flexible approach. Projects with a high proportion of reciprocal interdependencies will require great skill and effort in integration.

(b) *Differentiation:* The causes of differentiation between the contributors are shown by symbols representing the various types. As discussed in chapter 6, differentiation is caused by:

   (i) *technology* (or skill) - the technical demands of the job someone does, which determine the way in which work is divided between groups of people (T_1);

   (ii) *territory* (or location) - the geographical distance between people (T_2);

   (iii) *time* - the sequence of people's work on the project (T_3).

The factors creating differentiation can also be reinforced on construction projects by *sentience*. A sentient group is one to which individuals are prepared to commit themselves and on which they depend for emotional support. On the LRA it is identified as:

   (i) sentience arising from professional allegiance (S_1);

   (ii) sentience arising from both professional allegiance and allegiance to a firm (S_2).

The greatest degree of differentiation that can be shown on the LRA between contributors is therefore represented by the symbols T_1, T_2, T_3, S_2. The minimum is when there is no differentiation present in the relationship.

An examination of the degree of differentiation shown on an LRA will indicate the amount of integrative effort that will be necessary and in particular when and where on the project integrative effort is likely to be especially important. Conversely, areas of the project that should require relatively low levels of integrative effort will be revealed.

(c) *Decision points:* The decision points at the various levels of the hierarchy (primary, key and operational) are overlain on the LRA. When designing an organisation structure, the decision points have to be anticipated. This is part of the planning process and requires the close collaboration of the client. A particular skill is to ensure that the arrangement of contributors is appropriately designed prior to each particular decision. When used for analysis, the arrangement of the contributors relative to the decisions made is exposed for examination. As referred to previously, the decision points provide feedback opportunities which should be taken for the project to be completed successfully. They can be indicated on the LRA together with details of the control against which the state of the project's development has to be measured.

(d) The systems and sub-systems that make up the total project system can now be identified. They will overcome conventional professional boundaries and enable the project participants to visualise the project in terms of interrelated tasks and people rather than in terms of professional compartments.

An example of a small part of an LRA of a completed project used for post mortem purposes is shown in fig. 9.5.

MATRIX SYMBOLS
The symbols define the way in which job positions relate to tasks and are selected and defined to suit the particular needs of the project. Each relationship can be classified into one of four categories:

(i) a transfer function of input into output within the operating system;
(ii) a control loop function concerned with managing the operating system;
(iii) a contribution of input to a task, external to the operating system;
(iv) a receipt of output from a task, external to the operating system.

Examples of relationships appropriate to the construction process, derived from Cleland and King,[4] are now described.

(a)   Transfer function

'Does the work': This is where inputs to tasks are transformed into outputs from tasks in accordance with instructions. It is the juncture

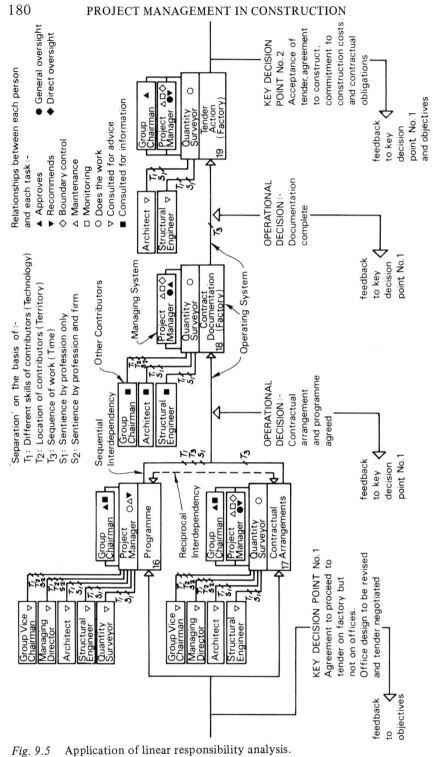

Fig. 9.5 Application of linear responsibility analysis.

of managing and operating systems where the output is transferred under the control of the managing system to be input to the next task. This relationship appears in each task box, and the total of the task boxes defines the operating system and those involved in it. It is the relationship in which professional skills are directly applied to the project, e.g. designing, constructing, preparing documentation, etc.

(b) Control loop functions

(i) Approves: This constitutes the final control loop function. The person in this executive relationship has the authority to approve the output of tasks for use in further tasks on the project. Normally, it is to be expected that the client will retain approval power for tasks directly affecting primary and key decisions, and that the member of the project team responsible for project management will approve those affecting operational decisions and other output.

(ii) Recommends: The person in this relationship is charged with the responsibility for making recommendations for approval of the output of tasks. The member of the project team responsible for project management will usually make recommendations to the client for approval. If the project manager is required to approve the output of the task, then some other member of the project team would normally make a recommendation to him.

(iii) General oversight: This is the broadest administrative control element and the source of policy guidance. The person in the direct oversight relationship responds to the wishes of the person in this relationship. The person in the general oversight relationship will not himself be exercising the skills of a task over which he has oversight. The primary role is to furnish policies and guidance of a scope that permits as much decision-making flexibility as possible within a task in arriving at the output. An example would be the role of a senior partner of a professional consultancy engaged to manage the project. He would not normally be working within the operating system but would be managing his firm's input and on these occasions would appear in the control loop as part of the managing system. The omission of the relationship from a control loop indicates that the task was assumed not to involve questions of policy.

(iv) Direct oversight: This is the administrative control element immediately below the 'general oversight' relationship. Although having no specific project functions, the person in this relationship has, and will exercise when necessary, the skills demanded by a task over which he has oversight. He is seen by others involved in the project to be maintaining a presence close to project activities. The omission of this relationship from a control loop indicates that the task was of such a routine nature that direct supervision was not necessary. An example could be a partner or senior assistant in a professional consultancy who is leading a team of people who are actually doing the work required by a particular task. The frequency of the appearance of this symbol on an LRA depends upon the level of detail of the LRA. Whereas it may not appear on an LRA prepared at a strategic level as it would be subsumed within the 'does the work' relationship in the task box, it would appear frequently if an LRA were prepared at a greater level of detail, say to plan the activities of one critical aspect of the project organisation which required close examination of a particular professional consultancy's contribution.

(v) Boundary control: When this appears in a control loop it indicates the specific control activity of ensuring functional compatibility within the task for which it appears and between it and other tasks. The person in this job position does not normally also have an administrative role. In addition, this relationship is concerned with relating the total system to its environment. It is a project management function as it is concerned solely with integrating the tasks and hence the people working on projects, and with ensuring that the tasks and the total system respond to changes in the project's environment. Omission of this relationship from a control loop indicates that the task is undertaken independently of other tasks in the operating system, which is an unlikely occurrence on a construction project.

(vi) Monitoring: This is the specific control activity of intra-task regulation concerned with checking prior to output to ensure that a 'does the work' activity is achieving its purpose. Omission of this relationship from a control loop indicates that it was not necessary to carry out such checks because there was total confidence that the activity would achieve its purpose.

Monitoring is a project management function. Although this activity may be considered to be the responsibility of the firm providing a particular contribution to the project, it is nevertheless the responsibility of project management to ensure that all aspects of the system are performing satisfactorily. Even if a particular task is receiving 'direct oversight' from a senior member of the firm providing the contribution, it is to be expected that the person providing project management would exercise a monitoring function over all activities.

(vii) Maintenance: This is the specific control activity of ensuring that a 'does the work' activity is being maintained in an effective state, both quantitatively and qualitatively, so that it is capable of achieving its purpose. Omission of this relationship from a control loop indicates that it was not necessary to maintain the 'does the work' activity. Again, this is a project management function concerned with making sure that the right number of people of the appropriate quality are employed on a task. As with the last relationship, even though the managers directly associated with the task may also consider that this is their function, it is also the responsibility of whoever is managing the total project on behalf of the client.

(c) Contributions to input:

(i) Consultation - gave instructions and information: This is an input of instructions and information to a 'does the work' activity and does not therefore appear in the control loop. Boundary control activities should ensure that the necessary people are placed in this relationship to appropriate tasks.

(ii) Consultation - gave advice and information: This is comparable to the last relationship but advice (rather than instructions) and information are input to a 'does the work' activity. Again, boundary control activities should ensure that the necessary people are placed in this relationship to appropriate tasks.

(d) Receipt of output

Output notification mandatory: This is placed in the output of a task when it is essential that the person in this relationship with a task receives timely information concerning a task output. The concept of this relationship is one of passive transmission of information.

BENEFITS

An LRA gives great visibility to how people work or do not work together on a project. In particular, it makes clear:

(i) *The sequence of the tasks and the effectiveness of the process in relation to the decision points and the actual decisions taken.* The tasks undertaken before a decision is made and the skills and status of the people contributing to the tasks and the decision will be clearly exposed.

(ii) *The type of interdependency, which identifies the way in which the tasks are related.* Inappropriately drawn interdependencies, e.g. sequential, which should have been reciprocal, are normally ineffective and most difficult to integrate (for instance, if the structural engineer and the quantity surveyor simply respond to the architect rather than each influencing the other's decisions).

(iii) *Who contributes to each task and with what status and what relationship to others.* More importantly, perhaps, it shows who does not contribute or who contributes in the wrong relationship. The LRA shows the degree of differentiation between contributors and hence the degree of integration required. The amount of differentiation is reflected quantitatively by the number of links between tasks and between job positions within tasks. The simpler the project the fewer links there will be. The links between tasks represent the differentiation that has to be integrated in managing the output of the tasks to realise the project. The links between job positions within tasks give the differentiation to be integrated in achieving the output of each task.

A qualitative measure of differentiation is given by identifying the proportion of each permutation of the factors of differentiation (technology, territory, time and sentience). Theoretically, it is possible to have any permutation of differentiation factors T_1, T_2, T_3, S_1, S_2), but in practice the configuration of the contributors limits the range which occurs on any project. For example, within a task the various professions in a multidisciplinary practice in which all members are located in one office and can only have a differentiation of T_1, S_1 (technology and sentience by profession).

It is to be expected that maximum integration will only be possible if an appropriate pattern of consultation has been established between the contributors. Such a pattern of consultation is demonstrated by all relevant job positions being in the 'gave advice' or 'gave information' relationships with each task.

Similarly, the degree of differentiation of the system will be a function of the pattern of consultation established. It is to be expected that differentiation will be greater as the number of contributors to each task increases as a function of the complexity of the project. This will, therefore, demand greater intensity of integration.

(iv) *Who exercises what management role as shown by membership of the control loop and who does not, but should do.* The control loops show the degree of continuity between tasks, particularly at decision points, and indicate the level of integration between tasks. The degree of integration exercised over the contributors to each task is identified by the activities of the members of the control loop.

Ideally the control loop composition should show continuity of membership. Normally, the member of the project team responsible for project management and a representative of the client organisation should appear in all control loops and should consistently exercise the same functions. Interruptions of continuity identify potential weaknesses in the integrative functions of the managing system. Interruption of the managing system between tasks in this way occurs particularly when the person in the boundary control relationship does not appear in the same relationship in successive control loops. Such discontinuity may be especially significant at decision points.

Duplication of management functions within a control loop may occur and represents split responsibility between members of the managing system. As well as being undesirable in itself, it also adds to the complexity of the managing system and can impair its effectiveness.

Control loop composition identifies the level of separation of the managing and operating systems. If this separation is not complete, a potential weakness in integration may occur as the objectivity of the person occupying dual roles may be in doubt. If the managing and operating systems are totally undifferentiated, there would be no control loops and all task boxes on the LRA would be occupied by the same job position. If the systems are totally differentiated, none of the task boxes would be occupied by any job position appearing in any control loop.

(v) *The integration of the client's representative with the contributors to the project.* The degree to which the client's representative is involved in the project is demonstrated by his presence in the control loops or other relationships. In addition it shows the type of relationship he maintains with the tasks, e.g. approval power, general supervision, etc. Consistency of the client's representative is also shown.

Integration of the client's representative and the project team takes place within the tasks and between them. Within a task it is shown when the client's representative appears in the control loop for the task together with the member of the project team responsible for project management. Integration of the client's representative occurs between tasks when the same client's representative appears in the control loops of successive tasks together with the same member of the project team.

SUMMARY

As can be seen, a particularly interesting aspect of any analysis or design is the composition of the control loops. On projects that use a project manager from outside the client organisation but with close involvement of the client, it is to be expected that all control loops will consist of two members, the project manager and the client's representative. It will be interesting to observe the structure of the control loops if the client's representative has to involve other senior members of the client's organisation at various stages, particularly at key decision points. Continuity may break down and the functions exercised by the duplicated client's representatives in the control loops will generate complex relationships. Although such situations may be unavoidable, the use of LRA to design organisations will enable them to be identified in advance and allow steps to be taken to minimise disruption of the management of the project.

When the members of the project team do not organise themselves positively for managing the project, it is likely that their representative in the control loop will vary, giving lack of continuity between tasks and erratic relationships between the members of the control loops and the contributors who actually undertake the tasks. This is often the case where a senior partner of a professional consultancy is involved in securing a commission at the early stage of a project and then transfers responsibility for managing the project to another member of his staff, particularly if he then continues to maintain an ambiguous role in relation to the management of the project.

The level of detail chosen for the individual tasks and job positions will depend on the purpose for which the LRA is intended. This can range from using it to draw a broadly based map of the whole of a large project down to the design of the way in which a small section of the work is to be organised. Users can pursue the aspect of particular interest to them by selecting and defining the relationships they wish to design or study by the use of appropriately defined matrix symbols. An important advantage is that an LRA can be usefully employed at a level of abstraction suited to construction projects, which are invariably of long duration with a great deal of aggregation of the detailed activities in the project plan and hence in the data available.

Naturally, any LRA used for design should be capable of being updated and amended in the light of changing environmental conditions. As with any planning tool, it should not remain fixed if conditions change, but should be used to anticipate problems resulting from such changes so that they can be dealt with in the most effective manner.

It should, of course, be pointed out that LRA represents a structural approach to project organisation and that just because the appropriate relationship of contributors, operating system and managing system has been established does not mean that the people involved will work well together in the manner intended, and that the project will be successful. Even if the best organisation has been structured, a fundamental aspect of success will be the quality of the skills brought to bear by the contributors and the attitudes and personal relationships that develop on the project. All of these aspects will be significantly affected by the personal qualities of the managing member of the project team. Nevertheless, the LRA approach should result in an organisation being structured to suit the particular project as the technique demands that the operating system, together with the decision points, are identified before the organisation is fitted to it. That is, the design of the organisation should follow definition of the task to be accomplished. This should give the project manager a sound basis for harnessing the behavioural characteristics of the people involved in the project to the benefit of the client.

PROJECT OUTCOME

The major problem of evaluating the effectiveness of any project organisation structure or any approach to designing organisations is that the success of the structure in achieving its objective can only be measured against the client's satisfaction with the completed project. What often makes this assessment difficult initially is the problem of deciding who the client actually is. For instance, is it the body which places the commission with the project team, is it the user, or is it even some other body, say one which is responsible for administering the completed building? This problem is often most difficult to resolve in the public sector, for example in the case of a hospital.

Even assuming the client can be clearly identified, assessment of the client's satisfaction has to contain a large element of subjectivity. The client's expectation at the very beginning of the project is that he will be fully satisfied with the outcome. The components of the client's satisfaction can be taken as function, including aesthetics, price and time, and he expects to get the project he wants at the price quoted on the date promised.

The project team's objective will be to provide what the client wants and to achieve this they will have to mitigate and harness environmental forces acting upon the project. The object in designing the organisation structure is to provide one which has the greatest capability to produce the project required within the environmental conditions.

Assuming that the people involved in the project have the requisite skills to carry out their work, the success of the project organisation in dealing with the project is the difference between the client's expectation at the beginning of the project and his satisfaction at its completion. The greater the uncertainty present on a project, the greater the opportunity for the achieved outcome to fall short of the client's expectation. If the client is completely satisfied with the project on completion, it can be said that the project organisation structure used was suitable for that project in those conditions and performed satisfactorily. The problem is in measuring any shortfall in client satisfaction adequately so that judgements can be made about the performance of organisations that do not produce projects that fully satisfy clients. This is particularly relevant to the value of comparative studies of different organisational approaches. Ideally, objective quantitative means are required for measuring client satisfaction and environmental forces but these are not yet available.

Nevertheless, it is possible to make an assessment, albeit relatively subjectively, of a client's satisfaction with a project outcome and of the strength of environmental influences.[6] This can be useful in making judgements about the success of project organisations. It is important to remember these issues when powerful claims are made in favour of certain organisation arrangements.

PRESENTATION OF PROJECT ORGANISATIONS

Increasingly, throughout the world, invitations to bid for contracts require bidders to submit details of their proposed organisation structure and approach to the project in addition to the bid price. Quite reasonably, clients wish to be assured that the bidder has a sound and realistic approach to the organisation and successful completion of the project. The problem faced by the bidder, assuming he can produce an acceptable strategy for the project, is that of convincing the client that he can organise successfully to achieve what he claims. Propositions that adopt a conventional approach will not necessarily be accepted on face value as many overseas clients will not be familiar with the style and terminology. Frequently, such an approach will not be compatible with the client's needs or the local environment. In many cases, a technique is needed that will explain clearly and convincingly to clients how the project is to be tackled.

Obviously, an LRA will not by itself fully satisfy the client's requirements but it can provide a powerful illustration to the client of how the bidder proposes to organise to carry out the project. It also provides a valuable focal point for the co-ordination of other documentation which will be required to convince the client that the bidder has the capability to complete the work successfully. For example, it is usual for the client to require details of the firms and personnel the bidder intends to involve in the project. Such descriptions can be linked to the LRA by cross-referencing their descriptions to their positions on the LRA. The LRA also follows the style of a network and if it is intended to submit network with the bid, this can also be co-ordinated and cross-referenced to the LRA. Such a package can look very convincing to a client and his confidence in the bid can increase, with a consequently greater chance of success.

The large variety of organisation approaches and contractual arrangements which are available and necessary to solve the wide range of different projects on offer throughout the world make it essential for bidders to adopt a creative and constructive method of putting their approaches to clients. The LRA can be used to illustrate any of these approaches because of its flexibility in being able to represent organisations at various levels of detail. It is therefore suitable for bids for construction only, for design-and-build bids and for design-only bids. It is particularly valuable for joint ventures as it will clearly show the aspects of the projects in which the various partners are to be involved. The definitions of the matrix symbols will be most important in such arrangements, as they will define the responsibilities and authority of the various participants.

A particular advantage of the LRA technique in the presentation of proposals is that it should explain to clients what their level of involvement in the project is expected to be. This can enable detailed discussions to be held with the client prior to the bid being submitted, which will be advantageous to the bidder in clarifying the client's requirements in terms of both the project brief and of his expectation of his involvement in the decision-making process and organisation of the project. If, upon receiving a bid, a client can clearly see not only the design and the price but also how they are to be achieved and what is expected of him in the process, he is likely to be assured that he is dealing with a professional and competent organisation.

REFERENCES

1. Von Seifers, L. (1972) *A Contingency Theory Approach to Temporary Management Systems.* Ph.D. Thesis, Graduate School of Business Administration, Harvard University.
2. Bennigson, L.A. and Balthasas, H.V. (1974) 'Forecasting Co-ordination Problems in Pharmaceutical Research and Development' in *1974 Proceedings of the Project Management Institute.* Paris: Internet.

3. Anon. (Jan. 1955) 'How to know who does what'. *Mill and Factory.*
4. Cleland, D.I. and King, W.R. (1975) *Systems Analysis and Project Management.* 2nd. edn. New York: McGraw-Hill.
5. Walker, A. (1980) *A Model for the Design of Project Management Structures for Building Clients.* Ph.D. Thesis, Department of Surveying, Liverpool Polytechnic.
6. Walker, A. and Wilson, A.J. (1983) 'An Approach to the Measurement of the Performance of the Project Management Process' in *Proceedings of the Land Management Research Conference.* London: Spon.

10 Postscript

TRADITIONAL MANAGEMENT IDEAS

There has been little reference to traditional management ideas in this book. Traditional management thinking was based on the batch and process industries, which have limited relevance to managing a construction project. The approach to managing the construction process, producing a 'one-off' item of great complexity and size, requires quite different ideas to be used. Traditional management ideas were based upon a functional division of labour and associated management, a hierarchical concept of superior-subordinate authority and responsibility relationships, and some 'principles' of management.

The process of construction project management cannot usefully accept these ideas. Increasingly, the process requires skills across functional and professional boundaries. In such circumstances the superior-subordinate relationship is not so valid: innovation and development of a project require interaction of peer group skills, which would be stifled by such rigid relationships. Although ultimately some authority has to make decisions on the project, the work undertaken prior to decisions being made and upon which decisions are based must be allowed to take place without constraints within the peer groups.

In addition to being generally inappropriate to project management, the traditional 'principles of management' are in fact not principles at all. A principle is a fundamental truth; the 'principles of management' are rules that have been distilled from experience and are not universally applicable. Some of them may contain ideas useful to project management, but each should be considered on its merits and not applied automatically. For example, the 'principle' of span of control, which decrees that a superior is only capable of supervising a limited number of subordinates, is hardly appropriate to a multiskill professional team.

However, many of the features associated with the conventional approach to construction project organisation may stem indirectly from traditional management thinking. The structure of the professional institutions associated with construction reflects specialist divisions of skill, and hence of labour and management. Many of the conventions used in the U.K., for example standard forms of contract, reflect this and give rigidity to project management processes, although they do serve other extremely valuable functions.

The conventional organisation structure has placed project management in a subservient position relative to professional skills. These skills are at such a high level that they have been assumed to incorporate management of the construction process. This pattern was able to survive when the environment in which construction took place was reasonably stable, but as it increased in complexity other methods of managing projects were sought. Such developments have taken place world wide, even where some of the influences were not so strong as in the U.K., e.g. professional institutions in the U.S.A. For example, the first management contract in Hong Kong was signed in 1982.

The predominance of the conventional method assumes that all clients place similar demands on the construction process. This, of course, is not the case. The industry's clients carry out their main business in a variety of different circumstances and it is the environment within which they exist that generates their performance expectations of the construction process. A client whose business is carried on in uncertain environmental conditions expects flexibility and inventiveness from the project team in organisation design, whereas a client in a stable environment may be more concerned with strict accountability.

What has emerged, therefore, is an explicit recognition, throughout the world, of the need for project management skills in their own right rather than as something which is subservient to professional skills.

As traditional management thinking had limited use, a new way of thinking of construction project organisations emerged - systems thinking. This provides flexibility in the design of project organisations. It recognises that project organisations should be designed at the very beginning of the process - no later than when the brief is drafted - and that each organisation structure should be based upon the nature of the task to be accomplished and the environment in which it is to be carried out. That is, organisation is a function of task and environment and not the opposite, as has been assumed when the conventional approach is used irrespective of the particular project configuration.

THE PROFESSIONS

The relative positions achieved historically by the various professions and their influence on the manner of contractor appointment and project organisations have made it difficult for new approaches to emerge unless stimulated by clients' demands for change. The professions have therefore achieved some degree of monopoly and hence a protected position.

The strength of the professions and hence the standing of their members arose through the establishment and maintenance by them, or in some countries by government, of standards of professional conduct and skill. This had the most beneficial effect of protecting clients against the unscrupulous and the unskilled but it also had the effect of establishing their protected position and created patterns of working that inhibited innovation, particularly in the management of projects. Professions concentrated upon the development of professional skills, in environments that were relatively stable, at the expense of project management skills, a situation which is strongly reflected in the education of architects and other professions throughout the world.

There is evidence that the barriers between the professions are being broken down as they seek to survive in an increasingly complex and competitive society. The need to protect clients from the unskilled and unscrupulous is still of great importance but should not be a barrier to flexibility in the design of project organisations. The professions need to continue to protect their clients yet themselves find ways to innovate. There is still a preponderance of projects organised conventionally and most innovations have been generated from outside the professions, notably by clients. The professions should adopt a corporate approach to the development of project management skills.

TRADE-OFF

The arguments for adopting the optimum organisation structure are strong but in practice there may be more powerful criteria which result in suboptimal structures being adopted. One may be the overriding need for the protection of clients; another may be the need to be seen to be achieving the minimum cost for a project, which results in the adoption of competition for the award of the construction contract after the design is substantially complete. Such a need for public accountability may restrict the choice of organisation structure and produce suboptimal structures, inhibit management performance and result in deficiencies in project outcomes greater than the advantages gained by satisfying other criteria. On the other hand, the client may consider that a suboptimal organisation design is not too high a price to pay for such perceived advantages. All aspects of the project's circumstances need to be balanced one against the other. The fact that organisation design is one of the factors should not be ignored. With ingenuity and innovation on the part of both the client and the project team, it may well be possible to satisfy what appear to be conflicting criteria.

PLANS OF WORK

An illustration of the way in which the professions' and industry's concepts of project organisations can ossify is given by the use of standard documented approaches, for example those often used by government and those recommended by other official bodies, such as the Royal Institute of British Architects' Plan of Work. They often represent sound general approaches to conventional working of the design team. However, new approaches to project organisation have often not been formalised and given the status of such standardised approaches, so that the structures laid down in the latter take on a charisma which is difficult to substantiate in practice. The limitations of standardised approaches stem from the fact that they often do not discriminate between the various needs of different projects in terms of the environmental influences exerted upon them or the inherent complexity of the project type. Although they recognise the need for adaptation of procedures to suit specific circumstances, they do not normally propose methods or criteria upon which this should be based. Adaptation of standardised approaches may be discussed but nevertheless their formality tends to dominate. As a result they may lay down a rigid pattern of stages and not make explicit the fundamental importance of decision points. Although recognising, by implication, the fact that decision points must occur, standardised approaches often assume that the positions of the points within the process are fixed, and do not recognise that they will vary between clients and projects. The result is that standardised procedures may build in potential for inappropriate design of feedback loops and not stress the need for the project team to advise the client on organisation design and on mechanisms for the integration of the client and project organisations.

The lack of recognition of environmental variability is often illustrated by the statement that the brief should not be modified after scheme design, which may not be in the client's interests. Also, an assumption frequently made is that tenders will be obtained on a competitive basis after completion of detailed information, and that a specific job position, e.g. the architect, will exercise both management and design functions. Such standardised approaches may cast the client in the relatively passive role of transmitting information to the architect at his request rather than being closely involved in his project. As a consequence, low integration of the client in the process may be implied, which does not recognise most clients' expectations.

This critique is not intended as a condemnation of standardised approaches to project organisation, which may be quite appropriate for certain circumstances, but to illustrate how 'official' approaches can harden thinking to the detriment of the professions' and industry's service to their clients. Such effects occur in all countries where those responsible for influencing organisation structures do not critically analyse proposals but simply promote one particular structure above others.

STANDARD FORMS OF CONTRACT

A further constraint upon the design of effective organisation structures is reliance upon standard forms of building contract, such as FIDIC forms, used internationally, and Joint Contracts Tribunal (JCT) forms, widely used in the U.K. Standard forms of contract presuppose a particular relationship between client, design team and contractor and subcontractors. Criticism is frequently directed at managers of projects who make alterations to the standard forms, on the grounds that the legal integrity of the contract as a whole may be affected by changes. Although this criticism is valid and it is unwise to make such changes without expert legal advice, nevertheless the need for such amendments is a symptom of the lack of relevance of the organisation and managerial concepts often implicit within standard forms. Again, standard forms are extremely valuable in conventional situations but inappropriate to innovative approaches. Ideally, therefore, if novel organisation structures and contractual arrangements are being made, a special form of contract and conditions will be required to suit the particular circumstances. The preparation of such a form of contract will naturally be expensive and time consuming and will require a high level of skill to be exercised in its drafting. However, this may well be a low price to pay for more effective organisation.

As an example of the way in which the standard forms dictate particular management styles, the JCT and FIDIC forms both determine a relatively passive role for the architect or engineer respectively (who are taken as being the client's representatives), and for the client during the construction stage of the project. For instance, the clause dealing with extension of time allows the contractor to extend the contract period on a number of legitimate grounds. Clauses such as this do not allow the architect or engineer to be dynamically involved in correcting deviation from the original project completion date and place responsibility on the contractor.

The use of nominated subcontractors is another significant organisational element enshrined in many standard forms of contract. Nominated subcontractors can create conflicts of allegiance and duplicated and conflicting management responsibilities. Although contractually responsible to the main contractor and therefore having to follow his instructions, nevertheless nominated subcontractors tend to refer directly to the architect or to whomsoever is managing the project on the client's behalf as that is where their appointment originated. Lines of communication can become confused and can bypass the main contractor to the detriment of the management of the project. It needs to be clearly recognised that the nomination of subcontractors or, even worse, the establishment of contracts separate from but operating in parallel with the main contract is likely to create significant management problems. The disadvantages have to be balanced against any advantages it is considered may arise from the use of the nominated subcontractor device.

CLIENTS

A key factor in the development of project management is the attitude of clients and the professions' response to their clients' demands. Clients who build frequently are demanding a higher level of project management performance and the professions are having to respond by being prepared to innovate in order to satisfy the requirements of such influential clients. Although it would be more desirable for the professions themselves to stimulate new approaches, nevertheless influential clients can provide a much-needed incentive to the professions. In such circumstances professional advisers should take the opportunity to persuade their clients to organise themselves to enable the project management process to be effective. To achieve this the professions have to be prepared to 'get under the skin' of client organisations and to be more interested in how decisions that affect the project management process arise in their clients' organisations. With clients who are aware of the needs for sound project management, this should not prove to be unduly difficult. On the other hand, clients who are not so familiar with the construction process are unlikely to influence the project management approach adopted and initiatives will have to arise from the project team. It will be incumbent upon the project team to make clients realise that their organisation structure and the way in which they bring forward decisions that affect the construction process are fundamental to the project's success. This process of educating clients is a skill in its own right and needs to be developed by project teams.

There is a very marked variation in clients' perceptions of the construction process and their approaches to the design team, varying from a structured and formal approach to an informal and amorphous attitude, which tends to reflect the level of definition of their requirements. The project team needs to learn to cope with this wide range of approaches. For example, clients will need to be convinced of the benefit of an explicit and formally documented statement of their requirements at an early stage in the process as an essential component of a sound feedback mechanism. Clients may not realise that this is not confined to projects for which the client can clearly identify his needs but is equally necessary, if not more so, on projects with a high level of uncertainty.

Naturally, for the latter, the statement cannot be as detailed but will form an essential basis for revision and updating as the design develops. Similarly, action minutes of meetings are particularly important in uncertain situations. From these minutes information can be extracted for revising and updating requirements and for aiding feedback. Such activities are only likely to take place if initiated by someone whose primary concern is management of the project for the client and who is prepared to train the client in these matters.

The most difficult aspect of educating clients to the needs of project management is making them realise that it is very much in their interests to involve the project team at the very earliest opportunity. This has to be mainly a matter of general client education rather than being related to specific projects. The project team cannot insist on being involved earlier than the client decides. Perhaps the professions should mount a campaign in the technical and managerial press read by the major clients by addressing client conferences and approaching the bodies that represent clients. This requires a corporate approach by the professions, rather than one profession seeking to gain an advantage over others. Many clients who have little experience of construction are baffled by the industry and do not know where to go for truly independent advice on how to set about their projects.

EDUCATION OF THE CONSTRUCTION PROFESSIONS AND INDUSTRY

A major inhibition to the development of project management skills has been the conundrum presented by the education process for the construction professions and industry. Traditionally the professions and industry configuration has been reflected in course provision. That is, undergraduates have been educated in relatively watertight compartments which reflect their professional aims. Architects have done a course in architecture, engineers in engineering, etc. Graduates therefore emerge with relatively little understanding of the skills and contributions made by the people with whom they are expected to work in the project team. As long as employers expect a partly trained professional to be produced by undergraduate courses, the extent to which courses can be broadened is limited. To provide graduates with even a low level of professional skills during their undergraduate education is time consuming.

The inclusion of additional breadth in courses will require a reduction in skill provision which is likely to produce a strong reaction from employers. Within such constraints the educational provision for project management is likely to be a postgraduate activity. In many ways this makes sense because graduates, particularly those with some experience, should be better able to understand and relate to project management problems and issues. This argues strongly for part-time postgraduate studies in project management.

However, such a course would need to have a strong broadening component as well as in-depth project management studies. The greatest disadvantage to this approach is that by the time graduates enter such a course they will have acquired strong sentient associations with the profession of their first degree. It may be very difficult to unpick such allegiances, which may tend to inhibit sound development of project management ideas and applications. Nevertheless, such a pattern is workable given an array of options that allows students to acquire a breath of knowledge about the skills and contribution of other professions, followed by a penetrating study of project management ideas, techniques and applications.

A more satisfactory approach, which may be more possible in some countries than in others, would be to design and provide an undergraduate course common to all intending entrants to the professions and industry. Naturally, such a course would be broadly based and cover to some extent all the ideas, skills and techniques that underpin the professions and industry. Graduates would then undertake postgraduate studies in their chosen specialism, e.g. architecture, building, engineering, quantity surveying. One of these postgraduate specialisms could be project management. This approach would have the advantage of breaking down professional barriers as all would have taken a common undergraduate course and have an understanding of, and, it is to be hoped, a sympathy with, all the contributors to the process. In addition, those continuing on a project management postgraduate study would not be inhibited by allegiance to any particular specialisation. Even those who chose to take a postgraduate specialisation other than project management and then took a further postgraduate study in the subject would have the benefit of having done a common undergraduate course. Naturally, such a pattern should be linked to some professional/industrial experience at appropriate points.

This approach is constrained in many countries by the structure of the professions and industry. However, in some countries, particularly in the developing nations, such an approach has much to commend it. The result could be a far more homogeneous group of people responsible for and contributing to the construction process.

FEES

The question of fees is invariably raised in discussions on project management. It should be acknowledged that in most countries fee charges and conditions of service of professional consultants include management of projects for clients.

A project management fee in addition to the normal fees for professional skills to ensure that management is carried out properly would appear to be unreasonable. The cost of providing effective project management should be accepted as being included within the existing fee charges. An additional fee may be justifiable if special management services are to be provided that produce savings in costs in other areas, or if it can be shown that the existing fee levels do not reflect the management demands of projects in today's complex environment. The lifting of mandatory fee scales in the U.K. following the Monopolies Commission enquiry may lead to competition both in service provided and in fees charged. This could lead to considerable improvements in the fee structure offered to clients, with greater analysis of and concentration upon the management component.

A part of the design of organisation structures should be the negotiation of fees between the contributors. This should include the project management component, which clients should not normally expect to be greater in total than the normal combined fees of the contributors. It is accepted that this may be difficult to achieve against the background of conventional fee scale arrangements, but with the support and involvement of clients, negotiation in terms of payment based on the actual services to be provided should give an acceptable outcome. The calculation of professional fees as a percentage of the cost of construction means that the amount of work done by the various contributors for the fee paid is not known outside the individual professional practices. It is, therefore, difficult to establish the management costs of projects and whether an additional fee for undertaking this work to the extent demanded by today's conditions is justifiable. The level and distribution of fees for management of projects for clients relative to the actual time spent on management activities have not been examined but could be a fruitful area of enquiry if linked to an investigation of the management skills employed.

THE WAY FORWARD

The complexity of the environment in which many of today's projects are carried out presents a direct challenge to the inertia of the construction industry, its professions and its clients. The way forward requires greater recognition that:

- (a) Effective project management is fundamentally important to the successful outcome of projects.
- (b) Project management functions should in many cases be undertaken separately from the operational skills required by the project.
- (c) The initial function of project management is to design an organisation structure appropriate to the needs of the particular project.

In addition a more positive approach is required to the following:

- (a) The education of the professions' and industry's clients in the demands that the construction process places upon them.
- (b) The professions' and industry's willingness to understand their clients' organisations and what makes them tick.
- (c) The professions' and industry's response to clients' needs when conventional approaches do not suit.
- (d) The breaking down of professional and industrial barriers so that clients receive a concerted and co-ordinated approach to projects.
- (e) The education of members of the professions and industry so that they are properly equipped to carry out project management.
- (f) The acceptance that clients have a right to expect effective management of their projects within the levels of fee normally charged.

Index